DATE DUE			
GAYLORD			PRINTED IN U.S.A.

Emma and Eugene:
A New England Romance

A correspondence between
the Allen and King Families
of Vermont and New Hampshire

Kathryn E. King, Editor

december press

A special issue of December Magazine,
comprising vol. 40, no. 1, 1998

Emma and Eugene:
A New England Romance
Kathryn E. King, Editor

ISBN: 0-913204-35-8
Library of Congress Catalog Card Number: 98-73224

Manufactured in the United States of America

Cover photo: Eugene, Hugh and Emma, ca. 1904

Published by December Press
Box 302, Highland Park, Illinois 60035

CONTENTS

For Emma

"that social little body"

PREFACE

It's almost always the same story: You're looking through the effects of someone who's passed away, and in among the boxes, trunks, chiffoniers, etc., redolent of dust, faded perfume and cedar, you find them—the bundle of letters, sometimes tied with a ribbon, usually loose, the stamps on the envelopes (which might have had considerable numismatic value) torn or cut through, the address usually just a name and town, the postal stamp with town and state, a month and day, but no year.

Then you open one and begin to read. Ah! It's like commencing the study of Greek or Russian, the strange letters wholly unlike anything you've been accustomed to, the ink faded and blotchy, the spelling of the same word appearing a dozen different ways, and the punctuation resembling ink spattered off a toothbrush. Nevertheless, you're hooked!

A first reading produces little; a second and third, the same. Then, as you become more accustomed to how the writer shapes his or her letters, a subtle change occurs and you begin to comprehend just what the letter is about. At least, that's the way it went when I was going through my mother's belongings after her death in 1979. The letters were in a writing box that had belonged to my grandmother who died in 1944. My mother, who had never evinced the slightest interest in ancestors and genealogy, just packed everything up and deposited it to the top shelf of her closet and, as far as I know, never looked at it again. In a way I'm glad she didn't because then I might never have found the letters.

Part I is a correspondence between Huldah Smith Allen of Barnard, Vermont, and her niece, Mary Ann Waterman King of Potsdam, New York. Huldah was the wife of James Madison Allen, and Mary Ann of Benjamin Franklin King. The letters begin in the next-to-last year of the Civil War, 1864, and end in 1870. While the letters present a fascinating picture of rural Vermont farm life and a bit of local history, mostly they concern the families involved. They tell a complete—and poignant—story. Huldah Allen was a born, though unlettered, writer and I have not changed her spelling or wording. I have, however, cut some repetitious passages. Otherwise, the letters appear as originally written.

Huldah Allen was my great-great-grandmother. Her granddaughter Emma (my grandmother) married one of Mary Ann's sons: Eugene, and, in an odd but not unusual turn of events at that point in time, Mary Ann's

v

daughter Alice King became the second wife of Huldah's son Milton. Thus Emma's sister-in-law was also her stepmother!

Part II is a correspondence among several people: Milton Allen, his daughter Emma Bertha, his wife, Alice King Allen, Mary Ann King, and her son Eugene. It takes place in the late 1880s and 1890s after Emma has married Eugene and they are working in one of the several mills in the Vermont-New Hampshire area.

Originally, when I discovered the Huldah-Mary Ann letters I was going to publish them as one book, but when I found what I call the Emma-Eugene letters they seemed to fit together to make a whole story. Sort of tying up all the strands you might say. One could even put forth the argument that the whole story is actually about Milton and his family.

Since these were all personal letters to people who knew each other, there is very little explanation of just who is being addressed. I have tried to identify most of them. Several people, mostly women, have the same name and it was quite confusing when I first started transcribing the letters. For example, there are Alice King, Alice Abbott, and Aunt Alice. Alice King was Mary Ann's daughter, sometimes called Allie; Alice Abbott was Mary Ann's sister; and Aunt Alice was Huldah's sister. (Additionally there is a woman referred to in Part II as "Aunt Alice" whom I cannot identify at all. Also, one of Nancy Joyce's daughters is named Mary Ann.) I hope it will not be too confusing for the reader.

I have included a rather skimpy genealogical outline of the families, several of which were living in New England prior to the Revolutionary War.

I should point out that I am not a genealogical researcher and the outlines should not be looked at as anything approaching complete records. However, where an actual death record or marriage license exists I have placed an asterisk to indicate such.

I want to acknowledge the assistance of Alice S. Hagen, CGRS, of Burlington, Vermont, for her research on the earliest immigrant ancestors of the families, and Marilyn B. King, of Quartz City, California, for her assistance with the Smith and King branches.

Kathryn E. King
Washington, DC 1998

Persons Listed in Text, with Relationships

Part I

Hattie — Harriet (Waterman) Durkee	Mary Ann's sister
Madison — James Madison Allen	Huldah's Husband
Milton — Milton James Allen	Huldah's son
Eunice — Eunice (Smith) Campbell	Huldah's sister
Edwin — Edwin Campbell	Eunice's son
Sarah — Sarah (Smith) Campbell	Huldah's sister
Alice — Alice (Waterman) Abbott	Mary Ann's sister
Eldred — Waterman	Mary Ann's brother
Alice — Alice "Allie" King	Mary Ann's daughter
Benjamin — Benjamin Franklin King	Mary Ann's husband
Lewis — Lewis Smith	Huldah's brother
Martha E. Cass	Milton's wife
Mr. Austin — Edwin E. Austin	Martha's brother-in-law
Your mother — Mary "Polly" (Smith) Waterman	
	Huldah's sister and Mary Ann's mother
Christopher Waterman	Mary Ann's brother
"A cross, intemperate man" — Superan Waterman	
	Mary Ann's father
Alice and Edward King	Mary Ann's children
Emily Bullard Davis	A Barnard neighbor
Jasper Davis	Emily's second husband
Lucian Bullard	Emily's son
Charlie Durkee	Harriet's husband
Emily Bertha — Emma Bertha Allen	Milton's first child
Jacob — Jacob Campbell	Sarah Smith's husband
Lucy Keith	Jacob's second wife
Joh Abbott	Alice Waterman's husband
Nancy — Nancy Ann (Waterman) Joyce	Mary Ann's sister
Aaron — Aaron Smith	Huldah's brother
Eugene —Eugene H. King	Mary Ann's son
Hosea — Hosea Smith	Huldah's brother
Ira — Ira Joyce	Nancy Waterman's husband
Carrie Bell — Carrie Bell Allen	Milton's second child

Aunt Olive	Lewis Smith's wife
Son — Hugh C. Allen	Milton's third child; adopted by Edwin E. Austin and renamed Hugh C. Austin

Part II

Gladys Mary King	Emma's first child
Hugh Allen King	Emma's second child
Dorothy Emily King	Emma's third child
Helen Eugenia King	Emma's fourth child
Gramp	Benjamin F. King, Mary Ann's husband
Aunt Clara	This may be Mother Cass
Aunt Ella Cass	Mrs. James E. Cass
Clara Cass Hulett	Daughter of Emily and James G. Cass
Rolly and Ephream	Bascom House residents
Frank Hatch	Carrie Bell Allen Hatch's son
Hugh Austin	Emma's brother
Adelaide V. Huntoon King	Edward King's wife
Kate J. Davis	Hugh Austin's fiancee
Katie Bascom	Bascom House
Ernest A. Hulett	Clara Cass's husband
G. W. Huntoon	Relative of Adelaide V. King
Richard A. Hayes	Married Helen E. King
Charles Allen	Emma's uncle
Clayton Allen	An Allen cousin
Emma Hatch	Daughter-in-law of Carrie Bell Hatch
John W. Bowker	Florence King's husband
Fay N. King Adams	Wife of Nelson Adams & daughter of Hugh A. King
Richard A. Hayes, Jr.	Son of Richard A. Hayes & Annie Lees Hayes

[Editor's note: The words "lot" or "lotting" appear frequently in Part I. When Huldah says, "I don't lot upon your coming," it means that she wants to see her niece very much but doesn't want to get her hopes up that she will.]

Part I - Huldah and Mary Ann

My Dear Niece

Tis with the greatest pleasure that I find myself seated, pen in hand, writing to one whom I had almost given up as lost. For a long time I have been in search of you and the tidings was hailed with the livelyiest interest, when Hattie informed me that she had received a letter from you. I was happy to learn of the place of your residence. How oft at the close of day when seated in my little cottage has my mind wandered in search of those I love. Tis many years since we have seen each other, but let me asshure you that in rememberance you are ever presant with me. O what would I not give could I be permitted to see and converse with thee my child.

. . . Well it is now Tuesday and tis a rainy lonely day and I will finish my small sheet of note paper and have it on the way. I hope you may get it.

Harriet said she had written you some time ago but had not had any return from you when I last saw her. My health is not very good, altho I do my work. Uncle Madison and I are all alone in our little domicile as our all and only is in the war. He enlisted for three years the last time. He has been out twice before. Milton enlisted in the first company that went out from Woodstock, Company A, served his time out which was 3 months. Again he enlisted for 3 years, was gone 1 year and a half and was wounded in the arm at the battle of Fredericksburg and received his discharge. Again he enlisted for 3 years more and is now and has been one year at the front of the Rebel Capitol, Richmond. He was well a few days ago.

I generally have 2 letters a week from him. Milton is in the

1

3rd Vermont Light Battery and has been in front of the rebel works, in line, shelling them, for 15 days at a time. Then they were ordered back and others supported their place.

O my dear dear woman, I hope you may never know what it is to have a son in the war. And indeed this war is very sad to contemplate. In times of battle sleep forsakes my pillow, and I have no relish for food and all I do is to search the daily Boston *Journal* which we have evry night, and many many has been the time that I hardly dared to look at the list of killed and wounded, dreading to see the name of my own dear boy chronicled there. But many thanks to that Good Being, in whom I trust, he is yet spared altho he has shared in many a hard fought battle. O yes my dear and much loved Maryan the Lord is able to shield him from the deadly missiles of the enemy, and in Him is all my trust.

Perhaps you may think this rather a sad letter, but you will please remember that out of the abundance of the heart, the mouth speaketh.

Aunt Eunice is well. She lives with Edwin's wife. He is at the war, and Oscar likewise. And who is not at the war? almost evry one that is able to bear arms, but our Union must be preserved. It will never do to give up our liberties which our Forefathers toiled so hard to obtain. But it would be the most blessed tidings that ever greeted my ears could I hear the sweet notes of peace proclaimed.

Well I must think of bidding you a short adieu untell I receive an answer to this, then my dear girl shall have a long letter. I want to write you of Aunt Sarah's death and sickness but have not time and space in this. O I do so hope you will get this bit of a letter, and do return poor old Aunt Huldah an answer right soon.

I have just been reading a letter from Milton which come in tonight's mail. He is well. So I will close. My kindest regards to your dear husband and lots of love to yourself and children.

In my next letter I will write you more of what you would like to hear of our prosperity, and of Alice, for we live within three miles of each other, and of Emily and Laura.

Ever My dear Niece

Haveing been the happy recipient of a kind and affectionate missive from your hand, I will reply without further delay. I have four letters, unanswered, which were received before yours, and perhaps they ought to be answered first but I cannot see it in that light.

None from Milton however, for I answer my poor soldier boy's letters immediately and I have one a week and sometimes two.

What I was going to observe was that, my dear one, the beloved of my heart so far away from the home of her birth and no relatives to visit her, or to associate with, most asshuredly you shall be remembered by me, before all others, except my own dear boy.

. . . O I am so glad I have a new corispondent, and one whom I shall love to converse with well, altho tis by the use of the pen. Do you think you would know Aunt Huldah could you see her? I fear me you would hardly recognise her. This cruel and bitter war has caused me to grow old in my looks more in the past 3 years than I have for the past 15, still I have a secret presentment that my boy will outride the storm of lead and hail and return to his bereaved parents. The Good Being in whom I trust is able to keep and carry him through. O yes my dear and much loved Maryan I am striveing to live as a Christian should live. I cannot tell you how much I love my saveiour, He is the chiefest among ten thousand, and the One altogether lovely. I am striveing to be recconciled to His will.

You spoke of Aunt Sarah. O what a beautiful sight to see a Christian die. O that I was as good as what I think she was. She was a bright and a shineing example. She had her senses to the last almost, and the last words she said was, O see that beautiful pillow of light. O yes indeed she died happy and in the triumphs of faith, and I mourn her loss deeply. She was my counsellor and I dont know but I may say the best friend I had on earth. But she is now free from earthly sorrow clad in bright and shineing raiment, with a harp of gold in her hand singing halalujah to the Lamb forever, and Ever, and you and I must live so that we can meet her. Her text at her funeral, Revelations, 14.13, and I herd a voice from Heaven saying unto me, blessed are the dead which die in the Lord from henceforth, yea saith the spirit that they may rest from their labours, and their works do follow them.

She died August 23, 1860. I am 56 this next April, and Aunt Sarah was 3 years older than I. Aunt Sarah died with a cancer in the stomach. No earthly medical skill could save her. We employed the most able and skillful physitians of the day, but alas her time was come her work done, and verily do I believe she herd the welcome summons, Well done, thou good and faithful servant Enter thou in to the Joy of thy Lord.

And my dear Maryan, I know you will excuse me when I tell you that I have to lay down my pen and weep. O how I loved that sister, but she is gone as you say and our loss is her gain. As well, this is rather a sorrow stricken world when one thinks they are in a fair way to obtain happiness, it is pretty shure to elude our grasp. I thought when we come in possession of our pleasant little home that I would shurely be happy, but no, the war is robing our once cheerful firesides of loved inmates, and still there is a canker at the heart of many a Mother, and well do I know how to feel for them, full many a loved one has been brought home to be buried in the land of his birth.

. . . Another call for more troops, 300,000. Ah well they must have men to finish up this cruel war and I begin to take courage for the prospects certainly look brighter. Milton is 24 years old, and I want to tell you that he is Mother's own boy. Kind and affectionate and a very good boy to his Mother. O how my heart is bound up in my all and my only. He wrote me in his last letter that he thought he would come home in the month of January on a furlow. O I hope he will come, I would send you his picture but they have got them all away from me but one. If he gets more taken when he comes I will reserve one for you. I can send you grandpa's and I guess I will. He was a good old gentleman. I have none of my own, if I had I would sent it you. . . .

. . . and of all my nieces, there is not one that has so large a share of my affection as you do. Believe me, and when I come to gaze at your dear picture, I could not refrain from weeping. O how I wish you could come and see me. My home is pretty, my plants are just beginning to bloom, my window stools are full of house plants. My pets, I call them for I must have something to love and take my mind. And as I grow old I remind myself of Aunt Sarah.

Well tis sabbath day today and I deem it not amiss to finish my writing to one whom I love so well. I did not get a chance to send this to the office at Bethel yesterday. Tis 4 miles from here to Bethel post office and 4 miles to Barnard post office, but we have our mail come to Bethel because we can get our letters without going down on purpose. Always someone down out of the neighborhood and they bring up all the mail that belongs in this vicinity.

Well my dear niece I am going to work up a good lot of wool this season if I can stand it to spin. I make all of Uncle Mat's winter clothes, blue mixed shirts, and cloth for pants. Two years ago I made Aunt Eunice and myself each a flannel dress. O how warm they are in cold weather. I will send you a piece of them . . . Alice and her little boy was up here the other day, stayed all day. We had a good visit, and since that I have been up there to see her. I walked, tis one mile of leavel staige road. Was afraid it would make me sick, but on the whole I think it done me good.

Tis warm and pleasant today and it seems like spring and my hens seem to enjoy it by their noise, and they lay like smoke. What does Benjamin think of comeing to Gaysville? Does he want to come, does he read my letters. Tell me in your next letter. Give my respects to him and tell him that if he should come into this vicinity to reside, I shall be pretty apt to form an acquaintance with him for I never saw him, I regret it very much. . . .

5

Ever my Own, Loved Niece

Once more I am seated pen in hand and I am going to spend an hour each succeeding Evening untell I get my large sheet of foolscap paper written over. And then I shall send it on to one whom my heart loves most dearly. . . . Your last letter is received, with the lock of hair, and those beautiful verses. How applicable to my case, yes my head is beginning to be silvered o'er with the frost of many winters, but still, you would hardly perceive it.

My health is not good, as a general thing. In the fall and winter I am quite well and smart, but as spring advances and warm weather comes on then I commence to run down, have no appetite to eat, and I am shiftless untell cool weather comes on again. But I manage to do considerable work. Like poor Aunt Sarah, you know how industrious she was.

. . . I want to write you of my home. We own a farm of about 90 acres of land on a good road, a short distance off of the main staige road in plain sight. Ten minutes' walk will carry us on to the creek road where there is a sight of passing. There is a road that goes by our house direct to the other neighbours' but this other road I spoke of is the staige road that goes to Bethel from Woodstock. I had rather live a very little off than otherwise. It is a very pleasant place with good buildings and our house is a cottage house painted white. We have repaired since we bought here, new shingles, new clapboards, painted white outside and in, 4 windows fronting the road. We can see people constantly passing but not near enough to tell who they are.

We value our little home at fourteen hundred dollars. I am very much attached to my home. For our nearest Neighbour I have Edwin Campbell, Aunt Eunice's second son, and they are good Neighbours. In the summer time my little cottage is surrounded with roses.

. . . I read your kind letter many times. I write a great many

6

letters and there is work in it, but still I like to write to those I love and there is none that get so long letters as you do, you and Milt generally get a big sheet. . . . I had a letter from Uncle Lewis Smith a short time ago with his photograph. I expect it was a good picture but tis a long time since I saw him, and I hardly remember how he did look. . . .

March 30th 65

Good Evening my dearest Niece,

I resume my discourse again this evening. My old kerosine Lamp sheds forth a splendid light, and I have adjusted my glasses, and I can see first rate. O yes indeed, I wear glasses and have these five years, or perhaps more. I cannot read at all without them, and Uncle Madison weares them too.

Well I was going to write you of Milton. He has just been at home on 20 days' furlow, which caused my heart to sing for joy, and dont you think he made me a splendid presant, that of a new daughter. He married a young Lady in the town of Warren. She is 20 years old and Milton is 25. Her name was Martha E. Cass. I like her very well indeed. I had seen her some two or three times before when Milt has brought her home. Before he went to the war the last time and this time while he was at home on his visit he brought her home for good.

Yes my dear Maryan it seemed odd enough when she first called me Mother, and that was the same night she came. She is quite pretty and just as soon as I get Milton's picture, I will send them to you. I have hers now, but Martha says wait untell you get Milton's and send them together. He said when he got to New York he would stop there one night and if he did so he would have a lot of pictures taken and send them back to us by mail.

I hope we will get them, poor boy, he has gone back to his battery leaveing his little wife and poor old mother and father quite sad and lonely. Wish this cruel war was over dont you and perhaps it may end this season, people are prophecying it.

O how I do hope it will, before all of our dear boys are slain. . . . that morning he left our quiet little cottage was a sad one to us. O the bitterness of that parting hour, sad, sad indeed to the heart broken Mother, but sader by far to see the young bride of a few days, weeping bitter tears, with evry fiber of her heart torn, for the one she most prised of all the Earth. But as it regards the sorrowful parting of Milton, no tears, not a trace of any tears, no cloud upon his brow. And as he gave us his parting kiss, he bade us be of good cheer and droped words of hope and encouragement, full of bright anticipations that soon there would be no more war and we would meet in a few short months, no more to be seperated. And thus he left us. And poor old Uncle Madison, I thought it would well nigh crush him for he loves his only son, and only child, as only a father can. . . .

Not to worship my boy, but my dear Maryann, I wish you could see Milton. He is Mother's own boy, kind and affectionate and tender hearted, brought up tenderly, and Mother's word was always his law. And he never went any where but what he must bring home something to Mother. I am writeing now with one of his sweet gifts, and that is a gold pen. And methinks I hear you say, should think you might write better. . . .

I am so glad that I have found out the place of your residence, and that I can write to you, and believe me my dear one, aside from my dear boy and his wife, you come next in my affections, and ever will. Time nor distance can never erace from my memory that kind sweet face of yours when you took such untireing care of me at Norwich when I was so sick, and then when I got up with my little babe, how sick you was. You was wandering and out of your right mind, and would not let poor Aunt do a thing for you. . . .

Evening again, and my sheet almost done. Last night's mail brought us tidings of our soldier boy at the front, at Petersburg and Richmond, and he wrote that he was well, got there all right but did not stop at New York to have any photographs taken. I am sorry for I wanted to send you one and I will just as soon as I can get one.
. . .

You are going to have a letter from Emily soon. I was up there this winter and I carried up your last letter and she read it and said I am going to write to her, so I gave her your adress, perhaps you have already received a letter from her. We are all well as usual, the connection, and there is a lot of us and all settled pretty near each other. . . . Next time I will write of your mother so I must bid you goodbye untell you write again, remember my love to your kind husband and your children, and reserve a large share to yourself.

Barnard April 6th 1865

Ever my own dear Niece

Haveing received another dear letter from you I hasten to answer without delay. This morning I sent my promised Manuscript to the Office for you, and tonight I got a letter from you. Was glad indeed to hear again so soon from my loved one, . . .

It has been stiring times with me for the past ten weeks. Milton has been home on furlow and was Married in the time and has gone again, and I have been sick with this great cold, or rather distemper since he went away.

Well Richmond is at last taken and Petersburg. There is where my boy is and has been for more than a year right on the Petersburg line, and his Battery was in the battle of the 25th and he is acting Master of the pieces. Last night Martha his wife had three letters, and I two. He writes often, and he was not wounded on the 25, but they have fought many battles since, but we cannot find in our daily paper that his battery was called into position since the battle of the 25 on Fort Stedman. And my dear child, if my dear boy comes out all right this time, through all these hard battles, he may yet come home to his father and Mother and wife, which may the Lord in His infinite mercy grant.

O yes soon we hope to hear the shrill Clarion of war sounding the sweet notes of peace. Peace to our once distracted Nation, what glorious news that will be, will it not. There is great rejoicing throughout our northern homes at the fall of Richmond, the rebel Capital, the strong hold of the confederacy. Three cheers for General Grant, Sheridan, Sherman, and our veteran soldiers at the front who are winning for themselves a name that will never tarnish or grow dim, and the dear old Flag, which has been so near trailing in the dust, may it unfurl its bright colors and long may it waive over evry strong hold of rebbeldom. How thankful ought we to be to Him who giveth us the victory.

Well I have just looked at the faithful old time honoured time piece and it wants but a quarter to eleven. I read in the daily news untill nine o'clock then thought I would pen a few lines. . . .

I must close for I am some tired, am not well of my cold yet, have been haveing a bad cough but it is some better now. My new daughter is kind to me and the time is not far distant before you will have some pictures. But have got to get them taken first, and that is quite a task for me to go and sit for the artist.

I take a pinch of black snuff now and then. Do you ever think of Caleb Richardson . . .

Barnard May 26, 1865

My very dear Niece

Many thanks for your brief note which came to hand tonight and the picture safely enclosed within. O how closely did I study each feature of my dear and absent one, and I should say that it was a good picture indeed. How much you resemble your sister Alice. Uncle Madison thought it was Alice's picture when I handed it to him. I should say that you do look like Aunt Sarah some, and you have not changed so very much. You look as young as Alice does for her health is not very good and she has grown old in her looks very fast since she has been married. . . . shall put your likeness in safe keeping along with the rest of my treasures. Most asshuredly you shall have poor old Aunty's picture if I can ever get to Woodstock, which is quite a distance for me to go, 15 miles they call it, from here to the green. But I am going down this summer and you must wait patiently, and if Milton gets home you shall have some pictures then.

O how glad I am this war is over, but my boy has one year and six months longer to stay if they make him serve out his time. I am watching the mail now evry night for a letter from him, for he said in his last letter that he should know the next time he wrote whether he was to come, or serve longer. They have got to have standing armies you know.

What do you suppose they will do with old Jeff Davis? I guess he will have to swing on a sour apple tree. I was in hopes they would put him in to the Libby prison and starve him as he did our poor prisoners, but I think he will get his just due, hope so at any rate, dont you? He is an old rascal. I know we are commanded to love our enemies, but I can't see it as it regards old Jeff.

Saturday morning May 27th

Nine oclock my chores all done and now I must finish my small sheet. . . .

Martha, Milton's wife, is down to Bethel now staying with her sister as her sister's husband is in the war. She will stay untell Mr. Austin gets home, and they are looking for him now evry day. O what a glorious sight it will be to see our soldiers come marching home again. Happy thought that this war is so near its wane, but my dear and precious one we do not know but little of this bitter and fearful tragedy which has been enacted for the past four years. O how many desolate hearthstones, and how many broken hearted Mothers mourning for loved ones who can never return. It may be my lot yet, but the Lord is good in whom I trust and I lean upon His all sufficient Arm nothing doubting.

O my dear Maryan what bitter hours have I not seen. Once we herd that my boy was killed at the battle of the Wilderness. It sprung from a report that his name was read in the daily Boston *Journal*. It said L. J. Allen killed. We did not take the daily news then, and we thought it was so certain, but Emily and one of our neighbors, Mr. Bryant, went down to Bethel and they searched evry paper there was in Bethel and then came home. I saw them the moment they hove in sight. Old Em a good old soul came waveing her hankerchief and saying good news good news Aunt Huldah no such name as Milton's is to be found in the list of killed and wounded. I mourned one night and one half day under the mistake and then waited seven days, then came the letters four at a time and my boy was in that hard battle with his battery. He wrote me that the horses were hitched to the pieces or guns three days and three nights, and my dear one he came out unscathed, and many a hard earned victory has my beloved boy passed through. God in His infinite mercies be praised.

. . . Well I must draw to a close a thousand times obliedged to you for the likeness of your precious self. I have just been looking at it for the twentieth time and can hardly refrain from tears, so much does it look like the sprightly little girl of fourteen summers when you took such unceaseing care of me at Norwich. Forget it, no never, and I am looking forward to the time when you and I shall meet.

Do you know how far it is to where you reside, how many miles? Please tell me in your next. I do not know anything about Uncle Lewis' residence, only tis Adams, Jefferson County, New York. There is where I direct my letters. I should think you would hunt him up if he is anywhere near you, for they are very lonely.

They want we should come out there on a visit, would be pleased to if it was so that we could.

Well I will close, write when convenient. I shall do so shurely if Milton is relieved from this war before his time is out, or when the rest of the soldiers are he will be at home in the course of 4 or 5 weeks.

Barnard August 8th 65

To My Own Dear Niece

Again I commence to write, and it is a great pleasure to me to converse with those I love although it is through the silent language of the pen. I received your good and kind letter last eve. Was happy indeed to hear again from you and while reading the same it almost seemed as though my little girl was talking with me and you said you almost cried for joy that my boy was spared to me . . . Yes my own dear Child, I believe that I can say that I have seen a miricle in my day in the return of my dear boy from the war. 18 hard fought battles he has been in and some of them lasted five or six days. The Battle of the Wilderness for instance, besides being constantly on the skirmish line where it was equally dangerous. Blind, blind indeed should I be did I not see the hand of God in this thing, and O for the heart to love my Saveiour more and to serve Him better. I cannot express my feelings to you my loved one no better than by repeating this verse in the hymn book. What shall I render to my God, for all His kindness shown, my feet shall visit thine abode, my songs address thy throne. Yes and often do I sing this verse and I think I can say that I sing it in the spirit and the understanding. O what a good Being the Lord is, how I love Him for His mercies to me.

I am lotting upon the time when you and I can converse with each other face to face. Well my health is still quite good for I have had some help this hot summer. Milton's wife is an excelent

13

hand at house work and she has done all the washing and ironing, and a good share of other work and that has given me a chance to rest some and by so doing I may not get all tired out and run down. I take care of our milk, three cows, and that is some work, and I do most of the cooking. I have just commenced to spin. Martha does not know how to spin but she says she is going to learn. Am going to make a piece of flannel for shirts. Shall have it checked. Will send you a piece when it is done. Tis for the menfolks.

I am glad you have got some help. Alice you say is good to work. What a fine thing it is to have a girl of one's own then you can call to her to help you when you are nearly sick and feel that you have a wright so to do.

Well I have been thinking some time that I must write you about your dear Mother's last sickness. In the first place she had a felon on one of her fingers. It was very painful and she did not get any sleep with it for three or four nights. Alice was at home with her at the time and Harriet was at Lowell to work in the mill, and the first that Alice noticed anything rong with her was that she would keep takeing the wood out of the stove. And finally Alice said to her, why Mother, there is none too much fire and I want my clothes to boil, for she was washing. O well she said, the house must not be burned up, and so she kept doing. Evry time that Alice put in wood she would take it out.

And then she went down cellar and was gone so long that Alice went down to see what she could be doing, and found her pulling up the meat. She had got it all up and piled up on some boards, for Christopher had bought her a nice pig and salted it up nice for her just before going off to work, and she told Alice she was going to throw it all in to the river for it was poison. Then for a surety did Alice come to the conclusion that her mother was deranged. And she wrote to me to come soon as possible and see her Mother.

I remember it well. I had been takeing in some sewing and it come to two dollars, and so I took the money and hired me a team and took Milton and started. Milt was then 13 years old, and it was

14

before we come into possession of our nice little home. We drove down to Sharon as quick as we could. Never shall I forget how my dear sister looked, a sister that I loved most dearly. She lay on the bed when I went in but she raised herself up quickly, while her eyes shone with an unnatural lusture, and said Huldah I am sorry you have come. What did you come for? I said I have come to see you. Well she says don't you eat anything for evrything in this house is poison, the cucumbers are poison, and the rain water is full of poison and I beg of you Huldah, as you value your life, dont eat a mouthful in this house if you do you will shurely die.

I sat me down beside her and O how I wept. My dear dear sister I said bereft of her reason. Yes my dear Niece, I cried long and bitterly, I felt as though I could not give her up. O how meek and harmless she looked as she lay there, for her derangement was not of a malicious kind. She did not want to hurt no one.

Well after I had had my cry out I set myself to work to see if I could not convince her that she laboured under a mistake and when Alice got her tea ready I carried in a plate of nice victuals and told her there was not one bit of poison in it. This is what I brought home, Polly, and it is all right. She looked at the cheese and smiled, and I thought she was going to eat, but she finally shook her head and said no no I dare not eat it. So we set the plate down on the table and went out and shut the door, and soon we herd her eating. That's the way she always done Alice said. She would not eat before anyone. Then I tried to have her take a pinch of snuff with me, but she declined and said it was wicked for her to take snuff, but it was not for me.

She mourned a good deal about the sin that there was in the world and said I am the chief of sinners, and so I parted from that very dear sister after promising to come down again the next week. She kissed me and said I never shall see you again, for you will be killed going home, and I rode home with a heavy heart. Soon I got a letter from Alice informing me that Mr. and Mrs. Quimby had taken her to Brattleboro where she died in a few weeks, away from all her friends and connections. But God who is an evrywhere presant being

15

and who is an impartial Judge full of mercy and compassion is abundantly able to pardon and at the eleventh hour, do you not think so, my dear Maryann.

I cannot believe but that your dear Mother is very happy. She was a worthy person and one of the best of Mothers, only think of her hard lot, ten children and a pair of twins in the number. O how hard she toiled both early and late to bring up her little flock, with a cross intemperate man, and a man that was profane. What could any one expect of that poor down trodden Mother liveing in close contact with such a man, a man too that was an enemy to evry thing that was good and holy.

And then again we read do we not, that not evry one that says Lord Lord shall see the kingdom of Heaven. Far be it from me to believe that the Saveiour of mercy whom I love and adore would create a fellow being on purpose for misery, and if that dear Mother of yours who suffered evry thing but death, and suffered death at last, is unhappy in the life which is to come, she must have been formed on purpose for misery. Pardon me for I cannot see it in that light.

Yes my dear child, I am happy in the belief that the dear departed is now singing the songs of the redeemed, haveing her robes washed in the blood of the Lamb, where her tired and freed spirit now mingles with the countless numbers that surround the throne. O blessed thought. O glorious hope, to feel and to know that the blessed King of Kings should come into this sorrow stricken world and lay down His life as a ransome for lost and perishing sinners. Glory be to His name, and unto Him be all the praise for the Lord in His infinite mercy is able to forgive the penitent sinner in the twinkling of an eye. Nothing is impossible with God, and I have no misgiveings at all but what your dear mother is now free from all sorrow, with a harp of gold in her hand, clad in bright and shineing raiment. Yes my dear Child, where in my opinion she is far better off than you or I, and let us so strive to live that we may meet her where all is Joy and peace.

. . . It is now a whole week since I commenced this letter.

16

We have been haveing a good deal of company and work folks, and I have had to delay my writing for the want of time. Milton is building a new shed joining the house and we are going to have a nice kitchen to do work in, and then a woodshed and waggon house. It will be so handy to have a place to cook so that when company comes I can go away off into my little kitchen all by myself. . . . Milton has got some fotographs a finishing. They were not done the other day when he was down. I have not been to Woodstock yet but think I shall go this fall, when we get our work along so that I can leave, then I mean to have my likeness taken. I expect it will frighten evry one who looks at it. . . .

. . . I know it has been hard times with us here, so much taxes to pay that any one could not hardly get clothes to wear, much more think of journeying, but I hope the times will soon be better now that this bitter war is over. O how glad I be my dear one to think the sheding of blood is over.

Barnard, Oct. 22nd 1865

My Dear Niece

Once more I commence to write and hope you have not been impatient at my long delay, if so I will now make amends for my past neglect. I received your welcome letter containing the pictures with much Joy. . . . I should think that Alice resembled you. I can see your looks in her very plain. Please give my best respects to Alice and Edward and tell them that I thank them very much and still I am lotting upon your Husband's picture. I have often to regret that I never saw him or formed his acquaintance.

We are all in usual health which is quite good. Mine is real good this fall for me. No more bitter tears to shed on account of the sad and cruel war, and I am often reminded by my neighbours, that I have renewed my age since the close of our Nation's struggle, and I am inclined to believe it for I feel as light as a feather. There is such

17

a weight of grief removed from my mind. I often gaze at my returned soldier and think it nought but a miricle that he is here. . . .

Hello my dearest niece, yesterday I went up to visit dear Alice. I enjoyed a splendid visit. I have hardly visited her this summer on the account of our being so busy, but now our work is not so hard and shall have more time to rest and make some visits. I carried your pictures which you have sent me and we had a nice time in looking at them. Your sister Alice is one of the best of little women and is beloved by evry one, and is in quite good circumstances. How I wish you and your Husband could come and see your friend, and I think you will ere long.

Monday Eve, October 23rd

. . . Well I believe you spoke of Laura. She lives about 4 miles from us and we see each other often. Emily has married again, perhaps you knew it. She married Jasper Davis and they live close by Laura Morgan. Oscar has settled down in the same neighbourhood with them, while Edwin and his family live close by us, our farms join. Aunt Eunice is now down here with Edwin. I see her almost evry day. Laura has no children nor ever had any. Emily has had one by her second husband, a little girl, sprightly and O how pretty. She was seven years old, but last summer she died with diptheria. It almost killed Emily. Her son, Lucian Bullard, has served three years in the war and has come home unscathed to his Mother. Again I say God be praised, but many are the poor boys whose bones lay bleaching upon southern soil who have died martyrs to their country . . . but enough of this, it is too sad to contemplate.

. . . Our new building is nearly done, that is all that we are going to do to it this fall. Tis a nice building and Harriet's husband Charlie Dirkee was the master workman on the building. He is an excellent mechanic and a smart and enterprising man. We think a great deal of him. Milton paid him two dollars per day for thirty days.

18

My piece of flannel is just out of the loom and Martha is now makeing up the shirts for Uncle Mat and Milton. O yes Martha is an excelent hand with the needle. I spun the yarn for the flannel, and my dear one, will you believe me, I spun fourteen notted skeins in a day . . . and helped about the dinner and supper. Most truly I am much healthyer in mind and body this summer than I have been for the past 4 years . . . verily worriment of mind is more injurious to health than hard work.

Well, they have all absconded to bed, and left me and still I am writing. But with your leave I believe I will stop and have me a pinch of good black snuff—O yes indeed I love my snuff just as well as ever. Do you like it? You used to take a pinch with me now and then.

What do you do for stocking yarn, do you keep any sheep or do you buy your stocking yarn? Write and let me know. Does your husband work in the mill where he is at work?

Well my dear one, the said pictures are now ready and I will send them along. Martha's is a perfect one, but Milton's is not so good a picture as he had had taken. Our artist at Bethel is not a first rate artist. Milton has given away a great many pictures and some splendid ones, but this one is not a perfect one. Still we call it a good one it looks very well.

Barnard, December 28, 1865

My Dear Niece

Milton . . . has been blessed with a sweet little infant daughter, which is now five weeks old. Yes, dear Maryan, and I have done all the work right straight along, and have taken care of Martha and the babe and done all the washings. Do you not think I am smart. Truly I am so, and I am often reminded by my neighbours that I look 20 years younger than I did before the close of the War. . . .

19

Well my small sheet of Note paper is almost played out, and as it is now half past 10 o'clock, I guess I will hie me to bed and perhaps tomorrow Evening I will not feel so tired and shall conclude to fill another sheet. I want you to get the worth of the postage stamp. Good idea, don't you think so. Uncle Mat is snoreing profoundly, and Milt and Mattie are gone off to bed with their little pet, and Maryan, I want to tell you it looks like Milton, it has red hair and it is the prettiest little babe I ever seen, with Mattie's eyes. Tis a handsome babe.

How I wish you could step in and see me at this moment. I am seated at a table in one corner of the room, filled with plants. I have a variety of plants summer and winter. Our room never freeses in the winter, and they look so nice.

Sabbath Morn, Barnard Feb. 4th 1866

Ever my own loved Niece,

. . . I am not intending much of a letter this time for we are so very busy, but by and by you will get one of my old fashioned Manuscripts. . . .

. . . when the birds begin to warble their sweet notes, and the makeing of shugar is at hand. Our folks are intending to make a good lot. They are agoing to tap two shugar places for Milton has bought him a farm. It joins ours and their house is in plain sight. I can slip over there acrost in fifteen minutes. They are a going to take possession the first of March. Tis called the best farm there is in town. He pays twenty three hundred dollars for it. He pays one thousand dollars down and the rest comes in two hundred dollar enstallments, once a year. It looks like a great undertakeing to me but he is all ambition and says he can swing it. And I think he will if he has his health and Uncle Mat is smart as ever to work. They are going to work together just the same as usual no division in any thing. They are going to tap two hundred trees and I think if it is a good shugar season they will make some shugar. O what would I not give if you could come, you and Alice to shugaring off.

You spoke of your Carpets. I should think you had been smart to work to make 30 yds of rag carpeting. Yes I made me one, twenty three yards and I think it is a hansome one, no boughten carpets I have got. I have a good many braided mats and some are very hansome. You know they save a carpet very much to spread them down by the doors and tables, and some of my mats are very large.

I make milk bread. One cup of new milk warm from the cow and one half cup of boiling water. Stir in flouer as thick as soft cakes, and a little saleratus, set it in a warm place untell it raises then mix my bread and bake it. I do not understand salt riseings.

Our little pet of a babe grows finely and tis a sprightly pretty child. We call her name Emily Bertha. Martha put on Emily after her own Mother, and Milton put on the name of Bertha. Emily Bertha, how do you like it?

. . . I was up to see Alice just one week ago today. She has an infant son of a week old. Aunt Eunice is nursing her. She was quite smart and doing well. . . . Alice is a nice woman, I think a good deal of her. But there is no one of all your Mother's family that I love so dearly as my own dear Marian. Our hearts were so closely bound in that one short year that we dwelt together that time will never erace it from my memory.

I have got both of your papers, three in all. Good reading in all of them. Milt is now looking at the engraveings in the war paper and, Maryan, should you send any more, do not write on them, only my name, not even your initials. I had to pay 10 cents postage on one and 13 cents on the other. The postmarster said they were written on but I did not find any thing wrote on them but M.A.K. Put on nothing but my address. . . .

My own dear Niece

 . . . How oft do I picture to myself your little home and you
surrounded by your family, and always feel to call down blessings on
your head. And my dear and much loved child, I am aware that it
costs you something to keep up your corispondence with me in
writing, but I do so love your letters, and I sometimes think that I
could not feel any different were you my own daughter, and letters
when they come in, which is often at the close of day, when one is
tired with household duties, from those we love is a rich recompense
to me for all that I pay for stamps and stationary. Do you not think
so? Your little home is worth contending for and no doubt you have
to economise closely in order to assist your husband, who is toiling
early and late to procure this home. How unfortunate that you
should lose so much money. This is a deceitful world, or the folks
that are in it. There is no knowing who to trust nowdays, but I am
intending to drop in a little something into my letter for you, and
remember you will not be forgotten by Aunt Huldah. One of these
days, my Gold beads are yours.
    Emily said to me the other day, are you going to keep your
promise, you always said Mary Ann should have your beads. I told
her most asshuredly, my word was sacred, and other things beside
them too you will have. Milton's wife is a good woman, but her
folks are well off, and who is more worthy of a hansome keepsake
than my own dear Maryann. None that I know of.
    Well my health is not quite as good this spring. It never is so
good in the spring. I have worked hard the past fall and winter, but
I am all by myself now, Uncle Mat and I. Milton and Martha are
snugly established in their new home, and as you sayed it is best so,
for my work will not be half as hard.
    No new shugar yet, our folks are all ready, they are going to
tap three hundred trees. I should send you some but it would cost
more than it would for you to buy it there. It is now sabbath eve.

22

Uncle Mat sits reading. I told him what you sayed in your letter, and he says give her my love and tell her I want to see her. Uncle Mat is a very steady man, no strong drink around now. Verily my last days are better than my first.

Maryan, I am going to send you one of Milton's letters for you to read which he sent me while he was on the lines of Petersburg, and some time when you write you may drop it in and send it back to me. I treasure up all his letters and I have a large pile of them. He is a good boy and I think he looks pretty well. I did not call that picture of his a very good one. . . . How I wish you could come and eat warm shugar with me, you and your children, but vain the wish . . . you may write in the month of June, but that time I shall be ready to answer and tell you how much shugar we made. . .

Barnard June 22, 1866

My dear Niece

As this was the month I set to write . . . I have not much news to communicate. My health is not quite as good as it was in the fall and winter. I have worked hard the past year, harder than I will for the year to come, and there will not be so much occasion for hard work as Uncle Madison and I are alone by ourselves. Tis better so, for I love quiet.

Milton and Martha are well, and getting on finely. O what a lot of crops they have got in to the ground, six acres of tillage ground, corn and potatoes, besides their grain, oats and India wheat. Milt has one of the best farms there is in Barnard. They work together, father and Milton, just the same as ever, and when Uncle Madison works over to Milt's then I have a chance to rest, the same with Martha when they come back on to our place. Our little grandchild is well, and is a very promising child. O she is so pretty. I tell Martha that I am afraid we shall all love her too well, and my dear niece you remember how well I always loved little children.

23

Well, supper being over, I will again commence to write . . . Milton and Martha went up to the Morgan neighbourhood yesterday. They made their visit at Oscar's. He is married and they have one child, a boy. They all live there close together, Laura and Emily and Oscar. Aunt Eunice is at Oscar's now. She is a good sister, but not one bit like Aunt Sarah.

. . . I ment to have sent you some books and papers long ere this, but we have been so very busy that I could not get time to go to the book store at Bethel. I guess you think my word not good for much, but I have had my house to clean and soap to make, and you know how it is, but I can see that I cannot work as I could once. I am troubled with the rheumatism, but when hot weather comes I will be better.

Our folks did not make but six hundred pounds of shugar. It's enough, I don't want but three hundred pounds for my own use, and shall have old shugar when we begin to make new. I have been haveing a bad time with my teeth, have had the ague in my face, have had two of my uper front teeth extracted. I was sory to lose them.

Well my dear one, I had just finished my letter and was going to seal it when the long looked for come at last, your letter. . . . O yes your request shall be gratified. I will write you about Uncle Jacob. Have wanted to do this a good while, but did not feel equal to the task. No, Aunt Eunice and I did not have anything to speak of. Hard case for Aunt Eunice because she was poorly off for clothes. It was Aunt Sarah's mind, and finally she made her will and gave all her wearing apparel to us and all the neighbours understood it so, but we got nothing.

Barnard July 1st 1866

Well my dearest Niece

. . . I have not yet been up to see Alice. I have been going this week, and next week, this long time and still do not seem to get started. Her little boy was here to see me yesterday, he staid all day. He said his Mother had got a new baby waggon and she was comeing right off, he was going to draw the babe. O me, now I have got to stop writing for Laura and Emily have just drove up to the door. Uncle Mat has gone out to wait on them. Goodbye for today.

Well, Mary Ann, my dear good Niece, it has now got to be the 11th of July, quite a skip from the time I commenced to write, but I will now double my diligance and try to finish today, for I am all alone, all over to Milt's to work, and I am about sick, and I do not intend to do any work today. Shall read your letters, and look at your picture which you have sent me. . . .

. . . Well you spoke of Aunt Sarah, and to know if I had any keepsakes of hers. I am sorry to tell you no. Not that I cared so much on my own account but Aunt Eunice truly kneeded her clothes. Aunt Sarah made her will one day when I was over to see her. Aunt Eunice took the whole care of her, and so she told Eunice to go and get her things and bring them there, on the bed so that she could talk with us about them. And as Aunt Eunice kept fetching on garment after garment, while I sat holding her hand, and you know that Aunt Sarah had an abundance of wardrobe, sights of dresses, bonnets and cloaks and shawls and under clothes and stockings, and evry thing. And Aunt Sarah thought that she felt smart enough to make a division of the things that afternoon, but I cried so that she told Aunt Eunice to put them away.

I could not help it, the contrast was so great. I would look at that dear inestimable woman, and then at her clothes and then I would weep and wail and ring my hands, and Aunt Eunice told me afterwards that I kept saying, I cannot have it so O my God. I cannot have it so, and then I would walk out in to shed kitchen, and try to calm myself, but I could not for I had no command over my feelings.

Well Mr. Ashly herd me crying, and he did not know but Aunt was worse and so he come in, and he advised Aunt Eunice to take charge of all the apparel, and when the proper time come then she and I would share our beloved sister's clothes, and they were all

25

put away as ours.

Well, the dear good sister died and was buried. There was a large concourse of people at her funeral, for Aunt Sarah was greatly set by. They come to attend her funeral obsequies, the distance of thirty miles, and O what a day that was with me. The meeting house was crowded to overflowing, for I felt that my best earthly friend was gone. Text, Revelations, 13.14, and I herd a voice from heaven saying unto me, write, blessed are the dead which die in the Lord, from henceforth yea saith the Spirit, that they may rest from their labours and their works do follow them, and O what a discourse. The best sermon that I ever herd. Aunt died August 23 1860.

Well, to proceed with my narative, Aunt Eunice staid with Uncle Jacob untell December, and then he told Aunt Eunice that he was going to break up keeping house and was going to board with Joel Ellis. So Aunt Eunice picked up her clothes, her own clothes, and Jacob brought her out to Morgans, and in just four weeks we herd he was married to Lucy Keith. And it was so, and he lived with his third wife just four weeks, and he was taken sick and lived three weeks and died.

I did not go to the funeral, for I did not want to but Aunt Eunice and all her boys and their wives went. Well when the funeral was over, Aunt Eunice asked Lucy about our things that was there, and she said there was none there for us. Aunt asked what had become of them, and she said that Jacob gave them all to her and told her to keep them and she should.

So Aunt said no more, but it near about killed Aunt Eunice, so hard as she worked there. But Jacob paid her by the week for her work, but it was a wicked thing in that church member. So Lucy went off with all Aunt's clothes, and about twelve hundred dollars from Jacob's estate. So evry one that says anything to me about it I tell them that Lucy earned the twelve hundred for I would not have been obliedged to have slept with Jacob Campbell 4 weeks for the twelve hundred dollars. Fact, truth, yes sir, so you have my mind.

Well I am going to stop writing now and have me some tea. Do you not think that I deserve a cup. I am very much attached to my tea and snuff. Well I have had my tea and two boiled eggs, and I made out to worry them down. My apetite is very poor this summer.

I had four fleeces of wool saved that Uncle did not sell. I thought I would work up some but I am going to give it up. I am going to lay in for stocking yarn, so that if you should come to see me, that I could have some for you and Alice. . . . The 4th of July passed off very quietly with me. I did not go, and did not have much company. Milton and his father went down in the afternoon, Martha did not go. There was a great turn out around here, but they all got a wetting comeing home for it rained like suds.

Uncle Lemuel Gifford and his wife and Charles are dead. I write it for you know they used to be neighbours of your Mother's. Uncle Truman Newton's children are all married, Laura and Lucinda and Orvis and Joseph. The old man is dead, the old lady lives on the homestead with Orvis. Enos has gone west, he makes a babyish whineing nervous thing and a strong second advent. He and his wife got their robes all made and on upon a set time but the Lord did not see fit to call for them, so they had to take off their robes and lay them bye for a more convenient season, and I guess the Lord has not called for them yet for I have not herd any thing about it.

Barnard Oct the 10th 1866

Dearest Niece,

Well, dearest, it is now Autumn and cold weather is drawing near and it always brings work in its train and my health poor but I manage to do a great deal of work. But as Uncle Mat says, I am going to let the squirrel set and cock his tail. I am going to let my spinning go untell next May, then I will work up my pile of rolls for I cannot do it this fall and do my other work.

We are drying apple and Uncle Madison has a hired man for a month or two and they are gathering in their crops. I wish you

27

could be here. Such a lot of apples and the best fruit. Milt has one of the best farms in town, and our little farm yields bountifully this fall, and our men are burning a coal pit, and you will see there is a good deal of labour going on and it makes our work Martha's and mine hard. Milton gathered 5 bushels of the large kind of tame grapes the other day.

Well the other day Charlie Dirkee and Hattie and John Abbott and Alice and their children and Milton and Martha were all here. I set two tables together for supper. They said Aunt Huldah's children were all at home that day. We had a gay visit. I told them I was coresponding right straight along with you and they all said send her our love when you next write, so you may receive love from all.

Nancy I do not see often for I cannot get so far from home as that. She was here two years ago. I have not been to Uncle Aaron's this 5 years. Seth Campbell lives up to Derby almost to Canada line, is doing finely on a farm of his own, with a good smart wife and 2 children. I wish we could see each other so that we could do our talking by word of mouth do you not.

Well I am makeing grape preserve this afternoon and while the juice is boiling down my business is writing. I am going to put by some nice little delicaces for fear you may come and I shall not have any thing nice to treat you with. And now it is time for supper and I will bid you a short adieu.

Well my dear woman, when I left your letter to get my tea, I had company from Pomfret, a whole waggon load of folks, and they staid all night. So I put my writing by and it is now a week since I began to write . . . kiss those little boys for me and bye for this time.

Barnard Dec 27th 1866

Ever my own dear Niece

. . . This is a cold and selfish world, evry one seems to be engrossed with their own selfish motives. It seems as though it was worse since the war. Evry one is trying to make great bargains and to cheat and defraud all they can. But for my own part I want to deal justly and honestly with evry creature. And you enquired to know if I enjoyed religeon, and to deal frankly and honestly by you I must say that I do not belong to any society and tis seldom that I go to the center of the town to church, but if I know my own heart I will say that I am strieving with all my ransomed powers to have my heart right before God. Tis the heart that God looks at, and I love Him for His mercies to me and I love to read and sing to His praise when I am all alone. O yes, I feel that I am not a cast away.

Evening, and I again commence to write. I hope you do not think that my mind is occupied or taken up with the fashions or fine clothes of the presant day, no indeed far from it. Would you like to have me inform you of my wardrobe, well then my dear one the costliest dress I have is a delaine which cost 35 cents per yard. I have no silk dresses nor no costly clothes beyond delaines and calico prints. I do not presume to follow the fashions of the present day, it tires me to look on and see others follow them.

. . . And now I will tell you concerning my work. I do not work to accumulate property or for the sake of getting rich, but I work because I love to and then again I have more ties. I work for my children, we all love our children you know, and all that Martha and I do goes toward helping Milton and Uncle Mat. We lay out our proceeds in nesesarys such as tea, cotton cloth and groceries, and each of us a new calico print, and that helps them to save up their money to pay their intrest and taxes. And whether Milton will meet his payments this year all them I do not know. The poor boy works hard enough in all concience, and Uncle works as hard.

Martha dried one hundred pounds of apple. We have all been very industrious, and honest industry is praiseworthy in any one, do you not think so. Well I am very sorry that I cant send you some apples. I regret it very much, if you had ritten me early in the fall I should have sent a barrel, but now they are all sold and dried up. We did not put in the cellar more than 5 bushel for us Uncle Mat and I, and I guess the rats will eat more of them than we shall, they are makeing horrid work with them and they rot badly.

Aunt Eunice is comeing to stay with me three or four weeks and then I will have more leisure to do more as I am a mind to for she will chore around some. The days so short and the men want stockings and mittens and pants and roundabouts made. I do not know as you know what a roundabout is, well they are a sort of half way frock waist and sleeves gathered into a belt. . . .

We own our little home clear and free from debt, but I never tried to economise so close in my life and all for the sake of helping our boy. He served through the whole Campaign, four years he fought for his country in danger of his life almost evry moment of the time, and through the mercies of the Lord he was spared to return to his own loved Home with only one minie ball through his arm between the shoulder and elbow. It plagues him about work, still he will chop a cord of wood as quick as any of them, and now that he is settled down with his pretty family and is trying so hard to make himself a home, I feel it my duty to help him as a mother all I can. And I hope he will succeed and prosper, and live many many years to enjoy God's beautiful sunshine as a reward for his bravery, long life to the soldier boys, they seem near and dear to me all of them.

Yes, most truly do I love them, then on the other hand when I see those that tried to make believe that they were sick, that their lungs were affected to get rid of going and could not make it out for the doctors had to examine them, then they raised money and hired them substitutes. I say when I see such go past with their fast horses, I say to myself, drive on with your fast horse and buggie you are nothing but a sneak and a coward. Take your comfort while other poor boys bled and died to procure your freedom. Well, enough said about that.

I saw Harriet last Sunday, she was out to our house, she works in the factory. There is a large woolen factory at Stockbridge where she resides, and she makes 35 dollars a month. She hires her a girl to do her work and pays her nine shillings a week, and then she has a good lot of money left to herself. Hattie is very smart and is an

excelent weaver. I wish your husband would sell and come to
Stockbridge, he would do well in Gaysville factory as it is called. I
should visit you if you lived about here, I know, if I never went any
where else.

Barnard January the 2nd [1867]

Well, dearest it is now Evening 8 o'clock. Uncle Mat has
gone to bed and I will try to scratch off a few more lines. . . .
Yesterday was New Years day and Uncle and I went over to
Milton's and took supper with them and when I came home in the
Evening I got my bible and hymn book and read a long time then I
meditated upon the past year which is gone bye. I felt very sad and
lonely. I always feel thus when the old year goes out for I reflect
upon my short comeings and think how much of my time has ran to
waste, but the new year, O may the Lord be my helper that I may
improve more of it in perfecting His praise.

You do not know how much I miss Aunt Sarah. I used to go
to her always when in trouble and when I could not understand a
passage in scripture. She would make it so plain. O yes indeed she
was almost the light of my path, my councellor and friend beside the
best of sisters. It seems sometimes as though this world was almost a
blank to me I loved her so well, and to her I was equally dear. And
while speaking of her, I do not forget your dear Mother I loved so
fondly.

She was one of the best of Mothers so patient and uncom-
plaining, never weary in toiling for her little flock, the family of ten
children. I sometimes bless the Lord for takeing her home, away
from this cold and cruel world where sorrow and sighing never
comes. Aunt Eunice is a good sister in her way and I love her well,
but she is so different in her ways. She never manifests no affection,
perhaps she loves me as well as Aunt Sarah did, and your mother,
but I cant see it. It always seemed to me though that if any one
loved another truly and well, they could not help showing it, dont
you think so.

31

I think of you a great deal and when I am thinking of you I always see you as you was when you lived with me at Uncle Truman Newton's, a good little Girl as ever was. How much comfort we took in that large square toped house. Believe me, you seem more like a daughter to me than the child of my sister and the love and respect and kindness that you there manifested to me will never be erased from my memory.

January the 8th

Well my dear one there has been a long skip from the time I left off writing, but now I will finish this and have it out to the office forthwith. I have not sold my dried apple yet, and all I can get offered for it is thirteen cents per pound. What do they pay for good dried apple where you live? Tell me in your next letter, and I want you to write soon. I am going to send you a small box as soon as I can get round to do it. I have not spun my own stocking yarn yet, there is so much to do about the house and Uncle Mat has a hired man. Our menfolks are lumbering, three meals of victuals to get a day and the days so short.

You must not anticipate too much, you told me I might send you anything I had to spare, and if you will pay the express on the box I will endeavour to send you more than enough to cover the expence. I have wanted to send you something this long time . . . I do not think I shall get the box to trundleing before the last of February then the days will be longer and we shall be out of our hurry, or the menfolks will. . . .

Aunt Eunice is seventy-three years old, and is quite smart, but I cannot tell you your mother's exact age, I have forgotten, I am very forgetful. Aunt Eunice has not come yet, have been looking for her this two weeks. My love to Allie and the little boys, and especially to the little boy Eugene who thought my letters smelt so good.

Dear Niece,

. . . I intend to start my little box about the 20th of this month and you must not laugh at it for you told me that I might send you just what I was a mind to, and just what I had to spare. I feel almost ashamed of the small pittance but I believe it will do you some good, I hope it will at any rate. . . . I have been haveing lots of company of late and you know what that is I suppose, there is work in it but it is now quiet again and I am glad, we have a great many connections take it on both sides. . . .

Aunt Eunice does not come yet. You said my last letter reached you and found you in one of your gloomy days dear child. I know how to feel for you I have them often, and a letter from you at such times always reflects a ray of sunshine acrost my path. Poor dear Aunt Sarah used to have many, many such, she said evrything used to look so sad and melancholy. I have thought it was oweing to ill health and a nervious temperament, and if Aunt Sarah used to have those disponding days, such a good Christian as I think she was, we must deem it excuseable in ourselves for I think she was a pattern of piety for any one to follow. O how I miss her.

Wednesday the 6th

Evening, and I will try and finish this and send it out to the office. I have made out to spin 20 knots today and prepared three meals. Don't you think I have done well. Little girls need praiseing you know. . . .

I have not seen Alice this winter. I have visited her twice since she has been to see me and I am not going again to see her untell she comes here, for she is young and smart and her little boy runs alone and I think she could come if she wanted to. I was in hopes Alice would come up here so I could tell her of my little box that I was going to send you, and if she felt disposed drop in a token of remberance to you but as she does not come I shall not say, or send her any word about it. Alice nor Harriet do not seem to think so much about their elder sister as I should think they would, away off from all your connections and friends as you are, but I think the more about you.

Well I must hurry up my cakes, as Milton says, for I am to have three men here on the morrow to cook for I do not know how long they are to work, they are comeing to do team work, for father and Milt. My two children say father and Mother and so I have got to saying father with them. I love my children next to my Saveiour. Martha is a good daughter and I love her very much, but the grandaughter, O how pretty with her golden curls I think she is the prettiest child that I about ever see. I tell Martha that she is a lent treasure.

Tell in your next what the prospect is about your comeing to Gaysville, tis a business place and I think Benjamin would do well at that place as a mill hand. Well now you may look for the said box the 20th and if it does not arive you may be shure that the menfolks are so busy that they can not go down with it. Tis 4 miles to the nearest station at Bethel, and the menfolks are rushing their work along for next month. You know they have got to tend the shugar trees. What sights of work they have got on hand.

Barnard Feb. 16, 1867

Dearest Niece

I will sketch a few lines to inform you of my health which is some better than it was when my cold was so bad. These hard colds are very troublesome, they generally work in my system and head for two or three weeks and then settle on my lungs and I have a hard cough, and when I get rid of my cough I call it that I am well of my cold, and my cough is now about well. I cured it by takeing Whites Elixir and Baxters pain killer. They are an excellent medicine.

34

Well now what will I write. My little box is all ready to trundle and I am ashamed of it. I have said to much about it. I guess you will think it is great cry and little wool, but I have done the best I could with my other work which I have had to perform. I haint been out but twice this winter, been over to Milton's twice and tis only twenty minutes ride so you will preceive I do not go a visiting much.

I meant to have spun you a little more stocking yarn but I had company come and I set away my wheel and I have not had it out since only to twist what I had spun. I know you will laugh at those little old pocket books but I thought they might please the little boys, they will do for them to play with. . . .

O how I want to see you, and if you should come to Stockbridge to live you must make up your mind to visit me often, and Allie. I mean to have her society some. I do not want her to work, tis only her company that I desire. Dear niece, I want to see you to converse with you about religion. There is none of the whole connection that casts one thought upon the subject. They all go to balls and dances and when they come together they must play Eucre. That is a very fashionable game now at cards but I do not join them neither do I make any pretense to religion but I think the more. O I want to be good.

We are haveing a terrible icy time. The ground is almost bare, no snow of any amount and tis cold and very icy and bad getting about. And we have had some terrible freshits in the late thaws. They are haveing melancholly times at West Hartford, the river got damed up just below there and the water set back into the village and completely flooded the village. The water rose so high that it ran in at the tavern chamber windows, Williamson's tavern, and people had to leave their dwellings. The tavern keeper lost three hundred sheep and two horses and his hogs, and worse than all, his daughter who was just going to be Married was washed away in the flood of ice. And yesterday they had not found her body and this sad calamety took place eight days ago.

All villagers shared the same as it regards property, horses, cows and sheep and farming tools, and almost evrything you could mention was swallowed up in the vast flood of waters, but we have not assertained but one person drowned and that was the hotel keeper daughter. People from Barnard and Bethel and all about here are going down there to assist them in extricating the animals and other property from the ice. They go on the carrs free of charge so that they render assistance to the unfortunate ones.

O how I pity those unhappy parents. Could they but find the body of their beloved daughter how much it would relieve their distress. It was a terrible freshit and such a sudden change of weather that it froze evrything up in one vast sheet of ice. I am in hopes to hear tonight that they have found the body of the lost one but I am afraid they never will find her. Perhaps you will see the account of this sad afair in the papers. . . .

Sabbath Evening February 17th

Well I will finish this sheet and start it out. It lacks only three days of the twentieth and it is terible going, but I must get my little parcels down to the station some way. I do not expect my box will meet your expectations, I know you will be disappointed in the box but I cant help it.

You must write what you think about comeing to Stockbridge to live, it is only 4 miles from me and tis a pretty place, a business place. Harriet's man is building him a new house and I presume he would rent part of it to you untell you could purchace you a house and some land. Write what you think about comeing, and what Benjamin thinks about it. I never would stay there in Wegatchee no longer away from all your friends and his. O it would make such a pretty ride for me to go and see you. I should take up my little white pony with something good for my darling child and hie away to see you. O I am afraid it never will be so. It would be something too good for me to enjoy but I am going to hope on and ever. Let us not dispair but trust in the Lord, He doeth all things well if we could only think so.

36

I want you to shave up that cup cake of shugar and put some water with it and melt it on the stove and let them have it on their bread, it will make them a nice meal, those little boys I mean, and kiss them both for me.

Barnard April 13th 1867

My Dear Niece

I have recently received two letters and one paper from you, and I will now write you a good long letter to reccompence you for them, they were good letters. For the same I thank you, and the paper was a pretty little budget of reading it beguiled many an Evening. Tis sweet to be remembered, is it not. I am afraid you have begun to think I have forgotten you. O no indeed, far from it. I think of you a great deal. Would that I occupied your thoughts as much as you do mine.

How I do wish you could be here today for we are shugaring off and tis hubbub and confusion. Milton and Martha are here and the little granddaughter, and she is so pretty. She is prattling around me. I can hardly write for her but I thought if I did not commence I never should get my large sheet out to the office.

Well my dear and much loved niece how do you do this spring. My health is some better than it was in the winter, and Aunt Eunice is with me now. I don't know but she will stay with me all summer. I think she is real smart for a person of her age, and she is seventy years old and you can hardly discover a grey hair in her head.

How I hope you will come to Vermont this summer or fall perhaps, you had better come in the fall if you come for it is the season of fruit I know twenty dollars is quite a sum to pay out for rideing in the carrs these hard times, for I do not see as things are very much cheaper, flour especially, and my dear one I know what it is to economise. I have learned the lesson well. . . .

37

Well what next shall I write. This sheet is a large one, and my pen has a long road to travel yet but I can always find enough to communicate when writing to those I love. Hope my long letters may not weary your patience.

I have not seen Hattie Dirkee this winter as she works in the mill and she does not get much time to visit. Uncle Hosea has been sick over a year, he lives in this town. I herd he was failing fast. I am going to see him this week. Aunt Eunice and I are going tis only 4 miles from where I live.

I believe I have not written you since I sent the box. You said the things suited you. I [wanted] to pay the express bill on the box but depot Master said it must be paid at the end of the rout. I did not design to have the box cost you any thing. Nevertheless I hope the contents of the little box was worth what you paid on it. You praised my apple and shugar and it done me good to think my loved one appreciated my good intentions. I supposed that I sent you a pair of very pretty mittens but when I was picking up things after Milton was gone with the box I found them dropped down at the end of the lounge. I was so sorry.

Evening, April the 18th

Well it is again Evening and I will try and finish my letter. We have not made but two hundred pounds of shugar this year thus far and I expect shugar weather is over. We made shugar on the home place this year as Milton has sold out his large farm. It was too much, and uncle getting along in years and Milton not being very well. He was a good deal unwell all winter, his arm plagued him badly. You know he was wounded in the battle of Fredericksburg. They are home again. Milton is to draw a pension in May or June on account of his arm. He sold his farm well and has made something in selling, so my dear if you come out to Barnard this summer or fall you will find the happy family all together. I dare

38

not lot any upon your comeing for fear I may be disapointed.

Aunt Eunice is going to help me spin and weave some cloth for flannel sheets and some shirt cloth and I don't know but frocking for pant cloth. Martha is learning to spin and she makes it go well. I am not so tough as I was three years ago. I cannot endure so much as I could. Then still I am industrious, and try to do all the good I can what little time there is remaining to me.

O how I long to see you my own dear child. I want to talk with you upon religion. I feel that you could teach me in divine things. How beautiful you write touching passages of scripture. One place in particular in your letter it revived my spirits, where you quoted that passage where it sayed, come unto me, and be you saved, all ye ends of the earth. Most truly I believe you could teach an old deciple. How I love good Christian people.

Please excuse me my dear for delaying so long to write. I have had a great deal to take my attention. Milton and Martha have been moveing home and I have been very busy. Nevertheless I think of you evry day and night. . . .

April 20th

I will now try and finish this page and have my letter out forthwith, and I hardly know what to fill out this page with. . . . I am feeling a little sad today not from any known cause, but I often have such days, and I think they are good for me for it teaches me how frail I am and I sometimes think that they are meant for our good, for I always feel at such times to commune with the Saviour.

. . . Well I have not seen your sister Alice this long time. I suppose she has a good many cares. She has two children now, her youngest runs alone, and they have bought them a very pretty situation a pretty white cottage house and some land. Abbott her husband is a sort of mecanic. I want to see her very much. Martha was there on a visit town meeting day, and she told Martha she was comeing here right off but I have not seen her yet.

39

Well now I must close soon. My plants are played out, it was so much work to take care of them that I had my shelf taken down that was acrost the window and gave them away, all but an ever blooming pink and that has blossomed all winter. I had a fresha and a cactus and an oleander putuna and an amarilla and lots of them, a horse shoe geraneum. All gone but my little pinky no. 1, as I call it.

Evening, Barnard, June the 3rd 1867

Dearest Niece

A good long and very excelent letter from you has been duly received and read many times over. How glad I was to hear from you, and to know that you and yours were in the enjoyment of good health, and I think you deserve a good deal of praise for writing such a good long letter. How fast you improve in writing, practice makes perfect is the old adage.

I was much pleased to hear you had been makeing your home pleasant. It is hard work to white wash and paper the walls, but it pays for it is so sweet and pleasant afterwards. Martha and I have been doing the same kind of labour. I take comfort in makeing my home pleasant and cheerfull. O yes there is no place like Home, for Home is Home let be ere so Homely.

Well my health is quite good at the presant time. Aunt Eunice is now weaving my web of white flannel. 22 yds in length. She will get the web out tomorrow. It has all been spun this spring, and day after tomorrow she is going up to stay a while with Uncle Hosea. He is failing fast, he is just as Aunt Sarah was. A tumor or cancer in the bowels and he looks just as Aunt Sarah did. I was up there to see him last sabbath. O what poor frail creatures we are. Yes most asshuredly dangers stand thick through all the ground to push us to the tomb and strange that a harp of a thousand strings should keep in tune so long. I have felt so sad ever since I came home from seeing Uncle Hosea. How I wish I could see you my own loved child, to converse with you concearning the life which is to come.

I have not herd from Nancy of late. Alice has not been down to Sharon as yet to see her. I was not aware that Nancy and Alice had any misunderstanding. I think I should have known it had it been so. I have always herd Alice speak in terms of the highest praise of Nancy. I always knew that your sisters did not love Ira very well, but your brothers and sisters all of them love and esteem Nancy. Indeed I know it must be so, and as for myself I always loved and esteemed her, but have not visited her on the account or for the reason that Uncle Mat does not like Ira and he will not carry me there.

It is very rong to cherish hardness towards any of our fellow men. Life is short at best and I think it behooves evry one to try to do right. O I do so want to be a good Christian, but I am so liable to err, and I feel that within myself I can do no good thing. Remember me in your prayer dear one, for we read the prayers of the richeous availeth much.

Well today is sabbath day and the apple and cherry trees are white with blossoms. How pretty it is. I have just come in from takeing a walk, and as you observed once in your letter, I love to walk out and commune with my own heart and view the beauties of nature and to raise my feeble petitions to Him who is the maker of them all. How grateful I feel to Him for all His goodness and mercies to me. . . . My family is well at the presant time and Milton and Martha have just taken their little girl and strolled out for a walk. Indeed it is a beautiful afternoon.

. . . Aunt Eunice has gone up to wait on Uncle Hosea. I have not herd from him this week.

Barnard, July 14th, 1867

My Dear Niece

It is now Evening and the busy scenes of the day is ore and I deem it a great pleasure to spend an hour in answer to your kind and interesting letter which I have just now received . . . O how I

41

lot upon the sweet message of love which I always receive from my dear and absent one.

The house is very still, they are all fast asleep but me. Father and Milton have commenced haying and they were very tired and went to rest early. The little girl Emma wanted mama to go with her and so I am sitting here quiet and undisturbed and I am weary with my day's work and must soon follow their example. . . .

Again tis Evening and I have replenished my Lamp and it gives a brilliant light. But my dear and much loved Niece, I have sad news to impart. You wanted to know how Uncle Hosea was and I have to inform you that he is dead. He died one week ago today of cancer or tumor in the stomach. O how much his sickness was like Aunt Sarah's. But my dear he has passed through what we have all got to sooner or later, and we are admonished daily, nay hourly that we have no abideing City but must seek one to come. And my dear one I am striveing O how sincerely do I want to live a good life or the remainder of my life and be a true and whole hearted Christian. And this Evening I am feeling so sad and to say the truth this world does not look much to me but I am industrious striveing to do my duty as a wife and a mother, aside from that the things of this world are all vanity.

Mary Ann, don't you remember in byegone days, years and years ago, you and I used to talk upon the subject of religion. I do not think that I knew half of the time what I was saying, or in what I believed, but now my views are very different. I think a person must be good and truly good to be a Christian, so much so that at times I almost despair of ever being one. Nevertheless I think and believe that Christ died to save just such a poor perishing soul as mine. Indeed I can say in all sincerity that I love Him for his great goodness and abundant mercies which I enjoy daily from His bountiful hand. Poor Uncle Hosea, how much he suffered, how poor and emaciated, nothing but skin and bone, and as I gazed at his sad remains I felt how much better it was to go to the house of mourning than to the house of feasting for there we learn our end. . .

Well this is my last page and it is nine oclock in the evening and they are all in bed but me. I prefer to sit up one hour later for the sake of converseing with you. . . .

You wished to know if Milton and Martha were to live with us always. Yes I expect they will. We have no child but Milton and here is his place with his parents. Martha is a very good daughter and a very worthy person and I love her well, but her health is not very good, not quite as good as usual. Her little girl will be two years old in November.

Your sisters are well at the present, except Nancy, and I have not herd from her this same time. Should presume that she is no worse. Please write and let me know how you prosper and whether you think you shall come in September. I think that was the month you said. I know it costs something to write so often as we do but never mind, we shall live just as long and I for one enjoy myself a great deal better to hear from my dear good niece often.

July 31, '67

Dear Niece

This letter has been written this long time. I thought Milton took it to the office at the time it was rote but he forgot it and it has lain in the clock this several days, but now I will have it out right quick.

Yesterday Hattie and her husband and children were here. She hoped you would excuse her, she said, for not writing to you. She also said that she meant to have written to you before now but her working in the mill together with the rest of her cares left her without one moment to spare. She sends love to you and said she would write soon.

O how I wish you lived near me. I do believe I should see you often. You will excuse my mistakes for the little Girl is prattling around me so that I can hardly write. How I wish you could see my grandaughter. O she is so pretty. We all love her too well. How can one one help loveing the little inocent creatures.

43

Only one month after this and July almost out, September will soon be here. I shall expect you to tell me in your next letter whether you come in September and if you conclude to come you write before you start and let me know when you will be at Bethel on what day and I will meet you there at the depot. I conclude that you can come through in one day. You told me not to feel bad if you did not come. No I will not lay it to heart. It seems quite a little sum to pay out, but dearest you have been away from the land of your birth a long time, and should you come I want you to come right here first and I will carry you to Alice's and to Hattie's.

. . . Martha expects to be confined in the month of September, but never mind, we will try and have a good visit.

Barnard Sept. 30th 1867

My Dear Niece

Tomorrow is the first day of October, and shall I have the pleasure of seeing one whom of all others I most wish to see during the comeing month. I presume you have thought it very strange that I have not answered your last letter but my time has been taken up, almost evry moment I might say untell this evening, and I am going to take time anyway to scratch you a few words.

Milton and Martha have been blessed with another daughter and it is now ten days old. And little Emmer has been haveing the whooping cough and has had it very hard. She is better now but they tell us she will have it eight or nine weeks. She has had it now seven weeks, and in order to not have the little infant have it I am keeping her out of the room where her mother is confined. Some of the neighbours say the babe will have it any way, but I tell Martha that there is nothing like trying the experiment.

So you will see I have just about as much as I can attend to. I am doing the work alone, with the exception that Martha had her Mother with her five days, but I am getting along finely. I am really

44

smart for me this fall. I am going to visit with you some if you come, shall go to Hattie's and to Alice's with you but I could not go to Sharon I do not think.

My work is all behind but who cares. I do not. If we are only well and Martha is quite smart. O I am all courage, if the babe only escapes the whooping cough we shall be very happy.

I shall meet you at Bethel depot as I told you if you come, and you must write when and on the day of the month that you start on. I suppose you come through in one day so your journey will not be very tedious. You said in your last letter that I would have to take you just as you was, that you should not fix up any. There is where you are wright, do not be to no more expence than your traveling expences, and remember that you are only comeing to your Mother's house, and then again I should hardly know how to receive a lady with a costly outfit. And further more, you must make up your mind that you are comeing among very plain and homespun people. We have none of the elegancies of high life, we live very frugal and simple and that is the way I like the best. I try to be thankful for the few comforts that I do enjoy, and I praise God from whom all blessings flow.

I must close, love to Allie and those little boys. Write if you come and write the day of week and day of the month so that there need be no mistake. I am lotting upon meeting you at the depot. I am comeing myself for I never could wait to let any one else go for you. Alice is lotting upon your comeing. . . .

Barnard, October the 17th 1867

My Dear Niece

I have just received your letter and I was so impatient to know its contents that I could hardly wait to break the seal. I was disappointed I must confess to think you were not comeing, but do not feel bad dearest the time will come before long for you to come.

45

Perhaps your husband does not know how to spare the money. The times are hard here with us, and money is hard to raise. I do not know the reason, but things are high and money scarse but we shall meet ere long, I feel it in my bones.

I said to Martha after reading your letter, O that I was rich. What would you do, go and see Mary Ann. Yes I said, I would start tomorrow. It gives me great happiness to know that you love me so well, and I will say it again as I have oft said before, that I have a good many nieces on both sides, Uncle Mat has a good many, and they all visit me and think a good deal of Aunt Huldah, or pretend to, but there is none, no, not one, that I love with such pure affection as I do my own dear Maryann and I had lotted upon your comeing but as you say we will visit yet a little longer by way of the pen which is a safe and trusty companion. . . .

You spoke about the girls not writing to you. I think it rather ungrateful in them and I have told them they had ought to write, but we all have our cares. No whooping cough yet. The babe did not taken it and I have accomplished my ends. I was bound the babe should not have it if I could help it. Martha is smart out in the kitchen and we are all well as usual. As for myself I am quite smart, only pretty much tired out. No easy places, as you spoke of I do not find, but Martha will have to take hold soon for I do not mean to work so hard much longer. . . .

Barnard Dec the 29 1867

My Dear Niece

Haveing delayed writing a long time, I will now try to make amends for past neglect. We are all well at the present time. My health is the best that it has been for 4 years. . . .

I am lotting upon your visit that is in anticipation as much as I dare to, for I have learned the bitter lesson that it will not do for me to lot upon anything. If I do I am shure to be disappointed, still I cannot help looking forward to the time with the livelyest intrest. You wished me to write when I wanted you to come. It does not make much difference with me, altho the months of August and July are very busy months with me for it is haying time and we keep our table set all of the time, lunch forenoon and afternoon with hot coffee. . . . I do not intend that work of any kind shall debar me from visiting with you. . .

Our little girls with their little red heads are well, healthy and fat as little pigs, and they are so pretty you will say so when you come. I love them too well I am afraid, and Martha's health is very good indeed for her. O yes, the prospect next summer for takeing comfort is greater if we have our health than it was last season. I hope it will be a good shugar season this spring. It was a poor season last spring, so that we can have lots of shugar to treat you with.

. . . It is sabbath Eve, and soon it will be new years day again how swiftly the time passes does it not, and if we only make good improvement of our time we shall do well, and if any is wise they will do so.

I have not seen Alice this long time, but just as soon as there is some snow Martha and I and the little ones are going up there. Alice has a good home and a pleasant one and Hattie has moved in to her new house. Her husband built it and Milton said it was a nice one evry thing was so handy. I have not been out there since they got into it. He has been to work on it all summer. O yes, the girls have done very well both of them and pretty families, but I do not believe that they lot half as much as I do upon your comeing. No doubt they will be orejoyed to see you, but I shall receive you as a Mother would her child, so let us trust in Him who doeth all things. . . .

My Dear Niece

I thought I would write a few lines to you. I have not written so long that perhaps you will be plagued to read it. I am looking forward to the time when I hope and trust we shall be permitted to meet once more. My health is good which is the best of all earthly blessings, altho I get very tired of my daily round of house work, but still I get along quite well. Poor Alice is gone and is at rest, and we do not know any of us how soon we may follow. O it is a great thing to die and if we are only prepared, haveing our work done and well done. I have thought sometimes it did not matter much how soon. . . .

We enjoyed Alice's visit very much, the girls speak about her evry day and wish they could see her. I tell them you are comeing and they look forward to the time as well as I, but I do not dare to lot too much upon your comeing, if I do I shall be shure to be disappointed. I do not allow myself to lot upon anything late years, if I do I am sure to get disappointed.

Uncle is well for him this spring, better than he was in cold weather. Nancy said Christopher's wife was very kind and sociable at the funeral. I hope she will remain so, dont you, how dreadful it is for relatives to live so at variance. . . . Milton and the girls and grandpa are eating warm sugar from off the snow while I am writing.

Barnard June 14th 1868

Dear Niece

I received your kind letter two weeks ago and was so happy to know that you had got nicely settled in your new home. Indeed it must be extremely pleasant for you to have your family all at home again. I begin to cherist hopes of seeing my own dear one again.

Forty miles nearer than you were before, that takes off quite a strip when any one is tired of riding.

Alice was up here last week and read a lot of your letters . . . she was glad you were a little nearer and I should not wonder if she and I should visit you sometime. I suppose we could go through in one day, but I am going to wait untell you visit me, which I hope and trust will be this fall. I think September and October are the best months to visit in, at least it is for me for then we are through with our haying and the produce needs no care untell it is time to harvest it. And then again the fruit is getting ripe and with all it seems the pleasantest time of the year for one to enjoy themselves in. . . .

I have been haveing some company, and who do you think my company has been. Let me tell you, Uncle Lewis and his wife, and I had not seen him for forty years. I did not know them, indeed they took me quite by surprise. I was very, very glad to see them, and they came straight through Potsdam, did not know that you lived there untell I informed them. They said they should call and visit you on their return.

They came directly here first and I have been up to Mr. Morgan's with them and they sent for Oscar and wife and Edwin and wife, and Aunt Eunice was there. Uncle Mat went with us and so you see we were the happy family. They are here now which is Saturday June the 13th. Next week Uncle Mat and I are going to share with them to visit Uncle Aaron's folks. Therefore I must disappoint you in my promised manuscript for indeed I can not find time to write it.

My health is not very good this spring. Lewis was disappointed in my looks, he said he expected to find me looking a good deal younger. I am in my sixtyeth year, next April I will be sixty, and for my part I should not expect to see any one looking very young and blooming at that age, should you. It is forty years since he saw me and I was sixteen years old. 40 years makes great changes in a person's looks, but I tell him it is longer than that since he was out here. . . .

Well Uncle Lewis and Aunt Olive have gone back to Adams, Jefferson County N.Y. they said if the carrs ran through your place in the night they should not stop, tis only eighty miles from where you live to Adams. They took the 2 oclock train, and that will fetch it night when they go through Potsdam. I have vsited untell I am all tired out. We have had a good many here and we have been out a good deal. Have been down to Sharon and we went to see Nancy. She was some better she thought. I told her what you wrote about comeing out and she was very glad indeed and I hope you will not give it up.

It is about 4 hundred miles from here to Adams, I think Uncle Lewis said, so you see your journey will be short in comparison with theirs. . . . Milton says he wishes he could see Edward and Allie. Uncle Lewis and wife came right to Bethel and then took the staige and walked up from the turn, which is a few rods from the main road. I took them to the depot and saw them start, and I supose they are at home now. Alice has visited with them. Well now I will close, but let me add I shall come and see you some time. . . .

Saturday Eve. Barnard, August the 16

My dear Niece

I have received your good and kind letter and was pleased to get an answer from you so soon. Always punctual you are to write to me. What a dear good child you are, how I wish you knew how well I love you, but as the old adage has it, actions speak louder than words, and should you be prospered in visiting me you will meet a warm reception.

Martha and I speak of your comeing evry day, and you now preceive that this is the month of August and the month half out and you bade me not to lot upon your comeing. O no indeed, for I learned the bitter lesson right Early to not lot upon any thing, if I do I am most shure to be disappointed. I know very well what it costs to live and it seems quite a little sum to pay out for the purpose of going a visiting, but after all you would enjoy it so much that I think you would feel more than repaid to see all your friends.

August 17th

Well my dear Mary Ann I will finish this now and send it out. I could not find a chance to close my letter on Sunday. We had company. She that was Martha Smith and her Husband they drove up to our door Early sabbath morning and went back to Sharon yesterday. She is newly married haveing buried her first man in the war. His name is George Scott, no one that you or I ever knew . . .

Milton and Martha went up to Alice's with Mr. Scott and Lady and had a good visit. Alice is looking for you, she has been cleaning windows and getting ready. I did not go up with them, I had rather wait and go when you come. . . . But if you should not come I will just say to you that I shall visit you before two years have expired if I am as well as I be now. One can go through in a day but Uncle Lewis said they should get in to Potsdam in the night. . . . I have had more of my own relatives to visit me this summer than I have before for 10 years, but none that will come quite so near my heart as thee my own dear child.

We are all well at home and our little babies have not been sick this summer. Pretty babes they are, I love them too well. I try not to but I dont see how I am to help it. . . .

Barnard Feb. 15th 1869

My Dear Niece

It has been a long time since I received your kind letter and I will now try to answer it, altho I cannot write you a long letter this time for I have been sick with the inflamatory fever. I am better now altho I do not do anything yet only to wait on myself a little. The physician said I had been a great while getting down and I should be

51

some time getting up.

I had ought to have written to you long ere this but have been putting it off. I often think of you and the good visit we had last fall. O yes I often live it all over in my mind. I am glad you had such a good visit with your friends at Sharon, and that your return home was a safe one and that you found your family all well.

You wanted to know about our work. O yes we dried three hundred pounds of Apple, and knit Mittens, striped and fringed ones, enough to come to nine dollars, so that with our apple and knitting we had about twenty five dollars to trade with. We bought us some calico prints, two a piece, and I bought me a dark brown one for hansome. It is not fitted yet, when it is I will send you a piece of it. Five dollars and one half a pattern. I do not feel like wearing it very soon but the doctor says he is going to have me better than I have been for ten years past. He comes to me now, I have been sick three weeks and I just begin to crawl around some.

You will way that I have worked too hard, and I guess I wont dispute you, but if I get up as well as I was before, I shall favour myself for tis wicked for one like me to work so hard . . . there was nine days that I could not set up hardly long enough to have my bed made but am better now, altho far from being well. Martha thinks I never shall be as well as I was before, but we cannot tell. Martha has been very kind and she has had a pretty hard time. I must stop now and rest.

Well I rested me a while and had a cup of tea and some crackers and I will try and finish this. I do not call it a letter but will write you again when I get well, if that is to be. I employ Doctor Sparhawk of Gaysville, he is called the best physician we have. He is a homeopathy doctor and I think he is doing me good.

Your friends are well around here. Our little girls are well and smart. Baby Bell runs all over the house and Lady Emma is a social little body. I do not feel much like visiting Potsdam at the presant time, nevertheless you may see me there some time. Our winter is fast glideing away, it will soon be sugar time.

We had a letter from Eldred a short time ago.

My dear Niece,

    With a sad heart I seat myself this beautiful sabbath morning to pen a few lines to you after so long a time. I have not written you for a long time I know, tis not because I think any the less of you, O no, but my duties and cares have been great and many, and now I can hardly do you justice my mind is so confused evry thing seems like a dream.

    I am with Alice today. I came up yesterday with my two little Motherless girls and we are writing together as she received a letter from you last eve. I received a letter from you some days ago and was thankful to get a few more lines from you.

    My dear, dear niece, how sad and dreary this world looks to me, my tears commence to flow as soon as I begin to tell you my loss. O how can I write it, it seems as though I could not have it so.

    Yes, poor dear Martha is gone, and is at rest. She was very sick through the whole of her confinement. She was taken with pains and vomiting and vomited through the whole of her sickness. The physicians, three in number, pronounced it child bed fever. She was very patient through all her sufferings. She was taken Friday night at 5 o'clock and was delivered the next Monday at two oclock and she died the next Monday at two oclock.

    O how I clung to her. I could not, and did not give her up untell the night before she died, poor dear woman, we had taken so much comfort together, and we loved each other so well. Our plans were all laid for the future and the new shed part was all finished off, a nice kitchen, a large bedroom at one end, a nice large pantry and nice square room over head with a large clothes press, and we were makeing our allotments upon takeing comfort.

    O dear, man can appoint but God can disappoint. O the utter desolation that I feel would that you could know. You wrote me in your letter to Alice that she must be all to me and how true. She is a dear good woman and she is now my all most truly. O would that I could see you for I love you just as well as ever I did, and tenfold better.

Will try to write you more punctual in future but you must think of my cares. The infant, a son, Martha's only sister has got it, has got a good home. Martha was put in the tomb at Stockbridge, in May her remains will be carried to Warren her native place and buried. This is a world of suffering and trouble is it not. O would that I was a Christian.

[1870]

Well my beloved Niece,

I am now at home. This evening Milton came up after me to Alice's. We had a good but rather sorrowful visit. How I love Alice she is so good and so feeling and so full of sympathy that I come home feeling somewhat comforted, but O my desolate home. And then again I do not know but I do rong to feel so for I have those two little girls to love and carress, and Milton and father, or Uncle Mat I might say, left to me which is far better I suppose than I deserve. But I had become greatly attached to Martha. She was so kind to me since I had my fit of sickness a year ago. This winter she has been like an own daughter to me.

My dear niece would that I could see you that I could tell you how desolate my heart is. O you can hardly imagin what a dreadful house this was, two doctors staid here all through her sickness. She had evrything done that earthly power could do and the neighbours were so kind. They would bake victuals and bring in for we were so distressed that cooking was not to be thought of.

O it was a heavy blow to us all. Milton is rather more reconciled of late but my heart bled for him. He will sit and look at his motherless girls and the tears will rain down his cheeks, and he will say O Mother Mother, what should I do were it not for you. Truly I am a woman of sorrow and acquainted with grief, but time the sweet soother of evry grief will in time I trust assuage our trouble. But as Milton says he never shall find another that will make her place good.

I have a young girl with me now but she does not understand house work very well. She has been with me one week. Girls are scarce. I have done alone except this last week. I shall keep her this, and then Milton says he has found a good one that will go right ahead with the work and she is comeing a week from today.

We have one hired man steady that does Milton's teaming drawing wood to Bethel four dollars and one half a cord and he goes twice a day and draws a cord at a load. We have a good span of horses, and our folks are doing a good deal of business, and I have done alone with the exception of this one week, for we could not find a girl. O how much I could tell you but I am getting very tired and must close soon.

Well my dear tis nine oclock and my little girls are in bed. Emma sleeps in her little crib bed moved up close beside mine and Claribel sleeps with Uncle and I, so you can see how my cares extend. Tis most too hard for me, still I am permitted to go through with it, and I do it without a murmur. One does not know what they can go through untell they are brought to it.

O dear how tired I am, I must stop and go to rest. My pen is poor and the ink is pale and had hope you can read it. Answer this dear, wont you. I want some of your good sympathy and counsel and I will try to write back again. I ought to write to Uncle Lewis and Aunt Olive, but when I shall I do not know. I try to feel reconciled and to think that the Lord doeth all things well, and I wish I was Christian enough to say Thy will be done, not mine. I would like your prayers for we read the prayers of the richeous availeth much. Farewell for this time and remember that I love you dearly.

My love to Alice, and those little boys. Come and see me again this summer. How I wish you could.

From your Aunt Huldah Allen to Mary A King

* * *

The death of Martha Allen split Milton Allen's family apart. Sometime during the months that followed a heartbroken Milton and his father Madison took off for the west. Both were attracted to hunting and the outdoors life and they looked about for a place to set down roots. There is no mention anywhere of the area they searched. From Vermont, the "west" could have been as near as Pennsylvania, or as far as Idaho or Oregon.

Huldah, on the other hand, also moved out of the Allen farmstead. She took both Emma Bertha and Carrie Bell to New York state; specifically, to Potsdam where Mary Ann and her family lived. Whether the Allens actually lived in the King household is not known, but the families were very close.

After about two years, Milton and Madison returned east, collected their family and moved back to the Barnard area where they had resided before although I don't know whether it was to the same house or not. Probably somewhere nearby.

For all her emphasis on health problems and protestations of lack of true religious fervor, Huldah somehow managed to pull herself together sufficiently to make a home for Milton's "motherless babes."

"Oh, I want to be good!" she exclaimed at one point. In the opinion of this distant descendant, she was.

Additional Letters to Mary Ann, and Miscellaneous Material

Letter from Nancy Joyce to Mary Ann

Sharon, April 21, 1856

Dear Sister

I received your letter some time ago and should written before but I have had to move this spring and had so much to do and my health is miserable this spring. I am all run down. You know what it is to have the care of a family and mine is quite large. I was glad to hear from you and to hear you had got along so well. It must be hard to part with your child but God knows what is right and doeth all for the best.

I have no news to wright. You wrote some to Christopher. He was gone to Ohio before I got your letter. Fore of the boys are their. Their is none but Eb and Eldred here and Alice. Harriet is at Lowell. We are all scattered. You wanted to know where father was, he has been in Sharon over a year. He works out and makes it his home to his sister Sarah . . . Eldred he is rather more stedy I think, he comes here quite often.

We live now in the village just this side of the mill, or you go down through close to the mill yard, a very bad place for children. I have them to watch and it is close to the river. I have to have a great deal of care. We did not expect to move but the place where we lived was sold and we did not want to go away back away from school. We shall send four to school this summer.

Alice works to Mr. Stertin's about two miles from here. She has not got any letter from you this winter. You wanted some of our dear mother's hair, we have not got any, we did not get any before she went away. I have mourned about it a great deal. When she was brought home in her coffin, her grave clothes and cap on, we couldn't get any. Oh it seems like a dream that our dear mother is dead. It seems to me that I could not have it so. If she had died here that I could see her and been near her it would been a great comfort but it is just as it was ordered to be.

I will send you the letter that came from Brattleboro to let us know she was dead. I have kept it sacred. I can't write much more this time, it is late and I can't see. You will be plagued to read it. My children are all well and Ira. I hope yours are the same. My love to your husband and children and accept a good share yourself. Write soon and often. Your sister

from N. M. Joyce

Edward sends Eddy his card. If you want to write to the boys direct your letter to Chillicothe, Ohio.

Letter from Edward F. King to Mary Ann

Madrid (Ohio), June 3 [1861-65]

Dear Mother

I will see now if I can write you a letter, though I don't think of much to write. I got my photograph taken the other day, perhaps you would like to see it so I'm sending it to you. We had a letter from Aunt Eliza the other day. Pop said he would send it to you. The last one of the Rose girls are dead, the funeral was here the other day. That makes two funerals there has been here since we were to home. I have not been to see Aunt Sarah yet and I don't know when I shall go. I guess Uncle John is mad, he has not been here yet to see us. We are coming home on the second of July if nothing happens.

I can't think of much more to write.

Edward F. King

Letter to Benjamin F. King from his sister Eliza

[1861-65]

Give my love to Mary Ann and Ed and Alice and the little ones. How is Thomas and is he smart. You must take him down here to see his grandpa. Tell Ed there is a young lady here that says she would rather see him than any body in the world. It is Miss Lyne Lyman. Does he remember her? Tell him that Chandler is a hunter. Don't do anything else for a living. Goes ragged and hunts muskrats and rabits. He is not smart but perhaps he will be some time.

The Widow Lyman is dead, died this spring. Dr. Allen is in the army, he is a surgeon and they need such out there now. Grant lost fifty thousand men in going fifteen miles on the way to Richmond. He won't have many left—after he gets there at that rate will he? E pluribus unum, one or many, unum confederatum. Old Abe is a tiger ain't he?

(Send this to Mary Ann)

Your wife wrote to me some time ago to know something about her brothers and sisters. I did not know anything then, but have since learned something. Nancy is still in Sharron, her husband has a small farm just above the village, some sixty acres and is doing well—and is said to be steady and industrious. Eddie Joyce is in the

59

army of the Potomac. Mary Ann is working out in the village for some one, the other three are at home. Nancy is well, Harriet is married and lives at Gaysville, Vt. I do not know her husband's name. Alice is also married and lives in this state some where. Her brothers are some of them in the war but I do not know which nor do I know where the rest are. She must write to Nancy and find out. John was at Sharron last week and saw them. Write soon and oblige.

Your sister Eliza

Letter from Nancy Joyce to Mary Ann

Sharon, Oct. 9, 1862

Dear Sister

I seat myself to answer your very kind letter I received some time ago and should written sooner but I have been sick. I am some better so I am about the house but not very smart. The rest of the family are all well.

I have no news to write of any importance. I had a letter from Eldred not long ago. He wrote that he was going to be married this fall and should not come to Vt. this fall. I hope he will get a good woman. I would rather he would settle here. I hope these few lines will find you and family well and enjoying your selves.

We had a letter from Edward Thursday. He was well then. I feel to be very thankful to the great and good Lord for His goodness to me and mine. He has spared our lives so long. I feel my unworthyness but I am trying to live so as to meet my dear friends in heaven.

I have not seen Harriet or Alice this summer. I mean to go out and see Aunt Huldah this winter. Milton her only child is in the army. Mary Ann is at home now. I do not know whether she will stay all winter. She wants to go to the factory to work. I want to see you and family and hope our lives will be spard to meet once more on this earth. If not, let us be prepared to meet in heaven. The children are going to church. They go to Sabbath school every Sunday. I do not go to meeting very often. I can't walk so far it is over a mild and we do not keep a horse. Ira is talking of selling the oxen and keep a horse. If he does I can go around more.

I presume you think strange that I do not write about Chris' folks. We had some trouble with them three years ago and we do not go there nor they do not come here, only to quarrel. I know nothing about them. Chris forbid me ever coming to his house or to look on him after he was dead. I am sorry to write it but I can't help it. I am afraid you will think I am very wicked but I have not misused them. Perhaps I have not done just right. If I have not I pray God to forgive me.

I can't write any more, the children all send their love to you and the children, mine with the rest. My love to Benj and accept a good share your self. From your loving sister

Nancy A. Joyce

Letter from Isabelle Joyce to Mary Ann

Sharon, Sept. 1865

My dear aunt

I now seat myself to answer your letter you wrote to Mother so long ago. I guess you will begin to think that we have all forgotten you, but it is not so. We are all well at present and hope you are the same. How are you getting along now? What is Uncle Ben doing now and Eddie and Alice, the little ones? I do not know though I long to see them and all the rest. We live on a farm now where we used to when you left.

Well, Aunt, my soldier brother is at home. He has been at home about 3 weeks. How glad we are now he is at home and how glad and thankful we all ought to be now this cruel war is over and the Union has the victory.

Well, Aunt, are you never coming to Vermont. You will be welcome any time. Mary is to work for Aunt Harriet. Ellen is married and I am at home helping Mother. Her health is better than it was when Edward was in the army, though it is not very good now. Tomorrow is the third day of the Fair and Edd and I are going down to White River Junction. If we see any of your Father King's folks we should not know them excepting John. He was at our house last fall and I think I should know him.

I should be very happy to have Alice write to me, I should be sure to answer it with exceeding joy. And you must write to me too, I like to write to relatives dearly and to hear from them too.

Mother is going to write you a long letter pretty soon. Uncle Ebb is over from the west now. Well I don't think of much more to write this time and I guess I have written all you will care to read. Your very affectionate niece.

Isabelle M. Joyce

Letter from Nancy Joyce to Mary Ann

Sharon, Oct. 29 [1866]

Dear absent but not forgotten sister

I seat myself to answer your welcome letter I received a few days ago. I was glad to hear from you and to hear that you and family was all well. We are all well as usual and Edward is well as ever he was. He was sick about one year and last spring we did not expect he could live but a short time. We thought he had the consumption but after he began to gain he gained rite off and now he is able to work and we are all very thankful. We are doing very well. We live in a poor house and have got to until we are better able to have a new one. We have 60 acres of land. We keep two cows, a yoke of oxen, a horse, a hog, one calf. We raise corn, potatoes, rye and buck wheat.

The children are all at home but Addie. She has gone up to see Ellen, her half-sister, you remember her she is married and got two children. You wanted to know about the folks, your old neighbour Andrew Willey. He lives where he did when you went away. He has got a new house built and has two sons married and he and his oldest son is in the store where . . . used to traid. I could tell you lots of news if I could see you.

Our brother Alic has been out here to see his brothers and sisters. He talked of comming to see you but had too short time to stay. We had a good time. I went up to see Hat's folks and Alice but we did not go to see Aunt Huldah. I had a real good time but it rained all the time we was gone. It is four weeks tomorrow since Alic started for the west. He said the boys was all doing well. I wish you could of seen Alic. He is smart now I tell you and as good as he is smart and good looking. I had not seen him for seven years.

I can't write half I want to, I will write oftener for the future. It is quite a job for me to write and if I do not set down and answer my letters as soon as I get them I am apt to neglect it too long. I have a good deal to do and my health is not good, but you write often and I will be more punctual. I want to see you and all of your family and hope I shall some time. Bell is going to write to you soon. We all send our love to you all. I will close by wishing you peace and happiness. Yours with much love

Nancy A. Joyce

Letter from Isabelle Joyce to Mary Ann

My dear aunt

I received your letter day before yesterday. I was so glad to hear from you. I love to get letters from you dear aunt, they are so good they make me feel so much better if I feel discouraged or weary. When I read them I feel ashamed of my weakness and go about my daily duties with renewed vigor. My darling Mother is no better. She is feeling very bad today. She thinks she will never be any better but I pray God she will. I try to do all I can for her. She thinks so much of your letters. She wants to see her dear sister so much she has got a new doctor. He thinks he can cure her so she has taken more courage. Oh Aunty, to have dear Mother restored to health would be joy unspeakable.

May is here today and her husband also. She has got a very nice man. He is so kind and good to her. His name is Henry Blaisdell. They board to the next place above us. They have been married some time. May is a little short chubby woman and he is a very tall slim man. They look queer together but can be just as happy for all that. She is most 19 and he is 23. A very suitable match.

You said you was not very well. I am sorry. What a blessing is health. You must doctor your self up before it is too late. Oh we shall all be so glad to see you. You will come as soon as you can. You must not work too hard but there is Alice. She is a great help and comfort to you I know. Tell dear cousin Alice I should so much like to hear from her to have a cousin to write to me. Is she not coming with you next fall? How I long to see her.

Alice nor Hat have not been down yet. I am expecting to hear from them now all the time, and Christopher I am sorry to say does not come to see her. He will go right by and not stop. Oh it is too bad. It makes her feel bad. She says if she has done anything to him she hopes God will forgive her if he will not.

Mother has been sick 7 weeks last night. It is a long and tedious illness but I hope she will be better soon.

Addie is at home with me. She is a great girl, most as large as I am myself. I got a letter from Uncle Alix yesterday. He is not very well. The other boys are well but have not written. Uncle William and Cousin Henry are here now. I can't write any more this time for I have got to write to Uncle Alix today. We all send our love to you and your folks. So good by from your loving niece.

Belle M. Joyce

Letter from Alice Abbott to Mary Ann

Barnard, May 8, 1869

Dear Sister

I received your letter a few days since. Was very glad to hear from you. I began to think some of your family or you were sick. You wrote you have been very poorly. I hope you are better this spring. It is very pleasant here today but it has been a long cold snowy winter.

Well I suppose you would like to know how we are getting along. We are all well. I am alone this summer as usual. John is to work to Woodstock and expects to work all summer. I have stayed alone most of the time since you was here. John worked in a carriage shop to Bethel all winter. We get along very well. John does not come home but once in two weeks for he has to drive a team as there is no one goes from this way that he can ride with. So I am very lonesome, dear sister. How I want to see you. . . .

I have been to see Aunt [Huldah] this week. I found her much better than I expected. Had a good visit with her and have been to Sharon the past winter and went to see them all. Nancy was looking the best I have seen her for four years. I hope she will get well again. I think a great deal of her. We had a good visit to Chris's and Uncle Aaron's. We are expecting Christopher and his family this spring. I have been looking for them today. Nancy's children have been up here to make us a visit since we were down there. We have been to see Aunt Eunice and Laura. They were very much disappointed to think you did not go to see them. They told me to give their love to you when I wrote.

In regard to father and mother some stones, I will do what I can to help get them some for I think it ought to have been done before. I think Alex would help. He talked of getting some himself when he was over the last time. It has been most three years since he was here and I shall look for him this fall. I am going to write to him. I think Chris and his wife was very kind to make you a present. I wish we all could done the same.

Fred goes to school. He sends his love to the little boys. He got a paper from them and was very much pleased. I have not seen Hattie for some time but heard her husband had gone out west to Minnisota and she works in the mill. As usual I do not think of much more to write. I think I shall go to see you some time. I am glad you had a good visit when you was in Vt. and want you to be sure and come as soon as you can again dear sister for I want to see you so much. Do write us often as you can and I will try and do the same. My love to Benj, tell him to come and see us when you come again if he can. Your dear sister

Alice A. Abbott

Dear Sister

 I seat my self this morning to answer your kind letter which I received and was very happy to hear from you and to hear that you was all well. We are all well at this time and hope when this reaches you it will find you all the same.

 We have left Chillicothe and moved to Lancaster 36 miles. I am running on the Columbus and Hocking Valley Rail Road. It is a new road, where is only 60 miles of track laid and we are running only 30 feet of that. The rest is not graveled up yet. Ebenezer is here on the road and Aaron is on a section 8 miles from here. He and family are all well. He has got two boys and two girls. Eldred is still at Chillicothe on the Old Road. They have one boy and two girls. Eldred was up here about 8 weeks ago. They were all well then. I have not heard from them since. William is out in the country about 30 miles from Chillicothe running a steam saw mill. He has got two children both boys. He has buried three children. His folks were all well when Eldred was up here.

 Well Mary Ann I suppose you would like to hear some thing about my family. I have got a good wife and two children, Alice and Albert. Alice is 11 and Albert is 8. Ebb is not married. I have a very good job here. I make about one hundred dollars a month. You wanted I should try and get Edward a job firing. There is no chance here just now but there will be when they open the other piece of road that will be about the middle of September. There is most always a chance on the old road where Eldred is. You might write to him. He might get him a place right away. Eldred has made a first class engineer.

 Well Mary Ann you spoke about father and mother's graves. I visited them when I was at Vt. last. I would like to have some stones put up to them. I will do my part towards getting them. You wanted me to come and see you when I go to Vt. again. I will but I cannot tell how soon I shall go out again. I promist the folks I would come out in 4 years from the time I was out last, that is, 3 years this September. I have not taken my family out to Vt. yet. I want to take them the next time I come out. Well I don't think of much more to write this time. Ella sends her love to you all. The children send their love to your little boys and all the rest. Give my love to Ben and the children and except a good share your self and write soon. From your affectionate brother

Alex C. Waterman

Letter from Alice Abbott to Mary Ann

Barnard, March 20, 1870

Dear Sister

I received your kind letter last night and was glad to hear from you for Aunt [Huldah] is here today. Staid here last night with her two little girls. Was very glad to see her she has not been anywhere before this winter on account of their sickness. She is a dear kind aunt to me. I think a great deal of her and mean to be a daughter to her now Martha is gone. I shall go to see her as often as I can. O how I wish aunt and I could stop in to see you, dear sister, how I long to see you.

Barnard, Vt. Feb. 11th, 1876

Dear Cousin

Happy was I to night to receive your kind letter & to learn you wer reasonably well. Your letter found us all better than when I wrote before. Colds will not generally always last but in this Sextion they have indured about all winter.

O Maryann how glad it makes me to know that we can sit down & talk with each other once again even with pen & ink & I think we shall both be the happier for it. There is such things as taking sunshine into our lives from others & I will not give up all of Gods sunshine, I am agoing to hang to it as tight as our President old uncle useless [Grant] did the Steers tail if it takes all Summer.

I do not know but it is gratifying Sometimes to always look on the Dark Side of everything, but I never got Gratifycation enough out of it probiley to look long enough to find the Chief Attraction. Do not think now that I do not considder poor health to that extent that renders it almost imposible to take any degree of comfort even providing any one would give you the chance, but Dear Cousin I tell you there is such things as invillids fighting back the oppressing Clouds & letting in the Sunshine & I think & know you have done it if mortal ever did & I am talking this to have you keep doing so.

I predict you dear little old Lady that your life is agoing to be different & for the better. More Sunshine more everything that goes to make life more desireable. So now cheer up if you should laugh right smart once in a while I do not think it would hurt you very much & I am affraid you would have to if I was arround & Maryann I should like to come to Endfield above all things for I want to see you all just as bad as I can but I cannot at present but will in the course of time. Anyway I will leave my team at Bethel &

come down on the cars & meet you at the Junction or Lebanon when you come up.

Oh we are lotting for that time to come. Tell Genie that we will go a fishing together if we have to take it when we got so old that we shall not be good for anything else, whether or no. Benjamin & Eddie I don't know, can't say as I am very much affraid of them. That is the greatest trouble with me, I don't scare worth a damn. Benjamin would be for sending visitors home would he not, Maryann? if I came down never mind, should not budge an inch. No, there is no man that I care to see any more than I do Benjamin & I liked him from the first & always shall & he can't help himself & I think & trust even that true friendship will be again established with us all, only on my part it never has been any different.

The same love the same anxiety for the happyness prosperity & welfare for you all & Dear Maryann it is the same with me thruout all the remaining years allotted to me by devine provedence. Friendship is but poor pay for the kindness you have shown to me & mine but it is of a kind that never slumbers or forgets & Time may yet grant a more earnest developement. Yes Dear Cousin I do appreciate you & deeply realize all that you have undergone & I am greatfull to God & his mercys that we have you left to us thus far & I am ancious every minute that glides away for fear that you will not be carefull & overdo, but take Courage from the Thought that in Allie one who will never falter in her love, dutys or Devotion you have a comfort & a Safeguard & equal to her love & tenderness to that Sick mother will come to her her Blessing & reward. I Bless her for it & ever Shall & although it comes from a source that may seem of no moment yet it is no less heartfelt, or sincere.

You wrote about my discernment of human nature. Yes I have been thrown almost from childhood among almost all & every class of people & common Sense had ought to have Teached me Something & if it has not experience has, & taking into consideration all that I have undergone & the ordeals which I have passed through I have every reason to rejoice & render thanks to heaven that I have come out so unscathed as I have & in the

70

purifying effects I have gained that which I should have not known had it been otherwise.

Well Dear Cousin I must not weary you any more this time & I hope this will do you as much good as your Dear & prized letter did me. I was so happy to hear from you Maryann if you deem this poorly written sheet worthy of an answer do not write to get tired take it by all jobs & fear not but what I can read all you write. So do not take any Paines to write good. Mother & all send love & good wishes to you all & say tell Maryann to keep up good courage & be carefull. Good Bye for this time. With much Love

Milton

Miscellaneous Material

Obituary of Milton J. Allen
(clipping from a newspaper probably in or around
Hill, New Hampshire, ca. 1904)

All over the country scattered here and there are a few of the men who went through some of the terrible battles of the Civil War. They do not talk much about it unless questioned but they can tell us of the fierce hand to hand fights, the desperate bayonet charges right up to the cannon mouth, the sickening sights of fields covered with dead and dying men, the long forced marches heavily laden with knapsacks and equipments and many things the present generation can hardly realize.

One of these heroes, Milton J. Allen, for several years a resident of the Hunkins road in this town, recently died at the age of 64 years. He was a Vermont man and served three months under the first call for troops from that state. On his discharge he reenlisted for three years, Sept. 29, 1861, in Co. E, 4th Vermont, and was immediately chosen as the color bearer, the most dangerous position in action.

He carried the colors through all the battles the regiment was engaged in and saw many of the color guard shot down at his side, but he escaped injury until the battle of Fredericksburg, when a ball shattered his arm and passed through one of the color guard killing him instantly at his side.

At his discharge he again reenlisted in one of the Vermont batteries and saw still more active service. Finally after several engagements, at one battle, the battery was in haste to get a position and the horses were on the run, when a wheel went over a stump throwing him off and crushing several of his ribs.

From these two injuries he became a wreck in health and has lived and suffered all these years. He was a quiet, humble man and rarely spoke of his terrible experience in the war. He was a member of the Daniel Lilly Post, G.A.R., of Vermont. He had been pensioned for many years and had applied for a total disability. . . .

Notice of Adoption
(probably from a Rochester, Vermont paper)

NOTICE.—Edwin E. Austin, of Rochester, Vermont, gives notice that he has adopted an infant son of Milton J. Allen, of Barnard, in said State, and of his deceased wife, Martha E. Allen, as his child and heir at law, and designates Hugh C. Austin as the name which he wishes said child hereafter to bear.

Rochester, May 9, 1870.

Obituary
(clipping from unknown newspaper, 1901)

Death of B. F. King

Benjamin F. King died Saturday at his home off East Pleasant street, aged 80 years. On the previous Thursday Mr. King fell from the second floor of his cottage at Webster Lake and the injuries and shock received hastened his death. The deceased was a native of Hartford, Vt. For the past 15 or 16 years he had been employed in the Franklin Mills. He is survived by three sons, Edward of Bristol, Eugene of Hill and Thomas of this city, and a daughter, Mrs. Alice Allen of Hill. The funeral was held Tuesday, Rev. C. U. Dunning officiating. Interment was in the Franklin cemetery. N. W. Perkins acted as director.

(Clipping probably from a New Hampshire paper, ca. 1895)

A Notable Gathering

An interesting gathering took place last Saturday at the house of Miss Eliza King on Maple street, it being the occasion of the ninetieth anniversary of the birth of her mother Mrs. Thomas A. King. Some twenty-five or thirty of the ladies of the Point who were best known to Mrs. King, assembled by permission, for a social congratulatory visit and supper, bringing many delicacies in the eating line, but more especially hearts full of friendship and good wishes for her who had seen ninety summers of the checkeredness of this life and always been a kind and useful member of society.

A very pleasant visit was enjoyed by all but to no one was it more pleasant than to the elderly lady. A very agreeable and glad surprise was the appearance of her son De Witt Clinton King and his son of Boston, who had come on entirely unaware of any gathering of the friends here. The company drank to the health of the hostess from cups over forty years old.

Mrs. King, whose maiden name was Sarah S. Rowland, was born in Lebanon [New Hampshire] in 1795. Her father, Wm. Rowland, was a soldier in the Revolutionary War, and her grandfather, Abner Smith of Middletown, Ct., was a captain in the same war. Her brother went as musician in the War of the Rebellion and died at Yorktown. Sixty-seven years ago she married Thomas A. King of Hartford, who died August 27, 1870. His father [error, it was his grandfather—Ed.] was also a captain in the Revolutionary War, under Montgomery in Canada. It was a patriotic family.

Mrs. King has lived here in the same house fifty-one years. Seventeen years ago the couple celebrated their golden wedding when a housefull, and even a yard-full, of people were present to tender their congratulations, but only four of them were present at this gathering.

Mrs. King has had eight children, five boys and three girls, one son being now dead. She retains her strength and faculties to a remarkable degree, and bids fair to be the hostess of a more notable event ten years hence.

CAPSULE GENEALOGIES

Allen Family

1. Samuel ("Samuel of Windsor") (b. ca. 1588, England, d. 1648, Windsor, CT) (came from Braintree in Essex County England, to Cambridge, MA, 1632, then to Windsor, 1635) m. Ann ___ (d. 1687)

2. Nehemiah (b. 1649, Coventry, CT (?), d. 1684, Northampton, MA) m. Sarah Woodford (b. 1649, Hartford, CT, d. 1712/13)

3. Samuel (b. 1665/6, Coventry, CT (?), d. 1717) m. Mercy Wright (b. 1669, d. 1728) probably in Northampton, MA in 1728

4. Ebenezer Allen (b. 1711, Deerfield, MA, d. 1760, Woodbury, CT) m. Eleanor Hurlbut (b. 1712) in 1732 [brother of Joseph Allen who was the father of Ira and Ethan Allen]

5. Elnathan [Rev. War vet] (b. 1752, E. Windsor, CT, d. 1827, Pomfret, VT) m. Sarah Gibbs (b. 1753, d. 1827, Pomfret, VT)

6. Roswell (Capt.) (b. 1777, Pomfret, VT, d. 1857) m. Belinda Pratt (d. 1854, Pomfret) 1802 in Pomfret

7. James Madison (b. 1809, Richford, VT, d. 1877/[1887], Barnard, VT) m. Huldah Smith, 1831 [see Smith Family]

8. Milton James [Civil War vet.] (b. 1840, Royalton, VT, d. 1904*, Hill, NH) m. (1) Martha E. Cass in Barnard, 1865 [see Cass Family]; (2) Alice King, in Lebanon, NH, 1876 [see King Family]

9a. Emma Bertha (b. 1865, Barnard, d. 1944*, Rutland, VT) m. Eugene H. King, 1889 [see King Family]

9b. Carrie Bell (b. 1867, Barnard, d. ca. 1944, Randolph, VT), m. Edward S. Hatch, 1885 [see Hatch Family]

9c. Hugh C. (Austin) (b. 1870, Barnard, VT) m. Kate J. Davis, Boise, ID in 1894 [see Austin Family]

Sources:
Allen, Wm. S., A Genealogy of Samuel Allen of Windsor, CT
Allen, Orrin P., The Allen Memorial, 2d series
Seaver, J. M., Allen Family Records (1929)
Himelhoch, Myra, Allens in Early Vermont (1967)
Vail, Henry H., History of Pomfret, Vermont, Vol. 1
Newton, Wm. M., History of Barnard, Vol. 2

Child, Hamilton, comp., Gazeteer and Directory of Windsor County
Additionally, some land records, censuses, and King family correspondence.

[Ed. note: Please be advised that these genealogies are not intended to be complete —
or even accurate, given the state of early records — but they might provide a good
starting point for someone to begin his or her family research.]

King Family

1. John (b. ca. 1628-29 England, d. 1703 Northampton, MA) to Northampton
    ca. 1645; m. Sarah Holton (d. 1683) in Northampton 1656
2. Joseph (b. 1673 Northampton, d. 1734) m. 1696 Mindwell Pomeroy (b. 1677)
3. Joseph (b. 1709, Northampton, MA, d. 1742) m. Mary Bridgman (b. 1714)
4. Hophni [Rev. War vet.] (b. ca. 1740-45, Northfield, MA, d. 1807) m. Joanna
    Holton (b. 1745) in Windsor, VT 1767
5. Asahel (b. 1769*, Northfield, MA) m. Lydia Alexander (b. 1766) 1788*
6. Thomas Alexander (b. 1792 Hartland, VT, d. 1870 Hartford, VT) m. Sarah
    S. Rowland (b. ca. 1795, Lebanon, NH, d. 1891, Hartford, VT) 1818 in
    Hartford, VT
7. Benjamin Franklin (b. 1821, Hartford, VT, d. 1901*, Franklin, NH) m. Mary
    Ann Waterman in Barnard, VT [see Waterman Family]
8a. Alice m. Milton J. Allen 1876* [see Allen Family]
8b. Edward m. Adelaide B. Huntoon in Lebanon, NH, 1885
8c. Thomas A.
8d. Eugene Harcourt (b. 1860, Wegatchie, NY, d. 1930*, Concord, NH) m.
    Emma Bertha Allen, 1889* in Tilton, NH [see Allen Family]
9a. Gladys Mary (b. 1893, d. 1894)
9b. Hugh Allen (b. 1895, Franklin, NH, d. 1974, Laconia, NH) m. Helen G.
    Kenney (b. 1898, Bristol, NH, d. 1986, Laconia, NH) in Tilton, NH, 1917
10. Fay Norma (b. 1918, Franklin, NH) m. Nelson C. Adams in Bristol, NH,
    1946 [see Adams Family]
9c. Dorothy Emily (b. 1901, Hill, NH, d. 1990, Rutland, VT) m. Lowell M.
    Wylie in Tilton, NH, 1919 [see Wylie Family]
9d. Helen Eugenia (b. 1904, Hill, NH, d. 1979*, Rutland, VT) m. Richard A.
    Hayes in Somersworth, NH, 1925 [see Hayes Family]

Sources:

> Early records, family correspondence
> Help from Marilyn B. King and Alice S. Hagen

Smith Family

1. Edward (d. Providence, RI, 1703) m. Anphillis Angell, in Providence
2. Christopher (b. ca. 1674, Providence, d. 1755-58) m. Mary Stephens (b. ca. 1677, Providence, RI, d. ca. 1726)
3. James (Lt.) (b. 1706, Providence, RI, d. 1755, Walpole, MA) m. Hannah Boyden (b. 1709, Walpole, d. 1759, Walpole)
4. Christopher [Rev. War vet.] (b. 1739, Walpole, MA, d. 1824, Pomfret, VT) m. Abigail Mann in Walpole.
5. Aaron (b. Walpole, d. Pomfret, VT) m. Mary "Polly" Leonard
6a. Mary "Polly" (b. 1799, Pomfret, d. ca. 1850, Brattleboro, VT) m. Superan Waterman [See Waterman Family]
6b. Huldah (b. 1809, Pomfret, d. 1877/[1874], Barnard, VT) m. James Madison Allen in 1831 [see Allen Family]

[The Smith family has some connection with The Prophet, Joseph Smith]

Sources:
LDS Records
Genealogical History of Rhode Island
Help from Marilyn B. King and Alice M. Hagen

Waterman Family

1. Richard (Col.) (b. ca. 1590, England, burial 1673 in Providence, RI) in US in 1623. M. Bethia ____ (d. 1680, Providence)
2. Nathaniel (bapt. 1637, Salem, MA, d. 1712) m. Susanna Carder in 1663
3. Benjamin (d. 1762) probably in Providence, m. Sarah Knight (or Mary)
4. Charles (b. 1705, Providence) m. Jemima Hawkins in 1729
5. Abraham (b. 1733, Johnstown (?), RI, d. 1818, Royalton, VT) m. Anne Brown (b. ca. 1732)
6. Gideon (b. 1764, Gloucester, RI, d. 1848, Royalton, VT) m. Sarah Lee (b. 1768, Bridport, VT, d. 1852, Royalton)
7. Superan (b. 1800, Royalton, VT, d. 1859, Sharon, VT) m. Mary "Polly" Smith [see Smith Family]
8. Mary Ann (b. ca. 1822, Sharon, VT, d. 1890*, Enfield, NH) m. Benjamin F. King [see King Family]

Sources:
  Genealogies of Rhode Island Families, Vol. II (1983)
  LDS Records
  Lovejoy, E., History of Royalton, VT (1911)

Hayes Family

1.   Henry (b. Ireland) m. Margaret ___ (b. ca. 1820, Ireland, d. 1880*, Manchester, NH)
2.   Henry H. [Civil War vet.] (b. 1844, Ireland, d. 1896*, Manchester, NH) m. Catherine Keefe (d. 1919*, Manchester)
3.   Walter Francis (b. 1878*, Manchester, d. 1956*, Manchester) m. 1899* Elizabeth Ann Solan [see Solan Family]
4.   Richard Arthur (b. 1900*, Manchester, d. 1978*, Lewiston, ME) m. (1) Helen E. King [see King Family]; m. (2) Annie E. Lees (b. 1903, Mossley, England, d. 1982*, Lewiston, ME) in 1931
5a.   Kathryn E. [Korean War vet.] (b. 1926) New York, NY
5b.   Richard Arthur Jr. (b. ca. 1936, Lewiston, ME) m. Carlene S.

Sources:
  Pension Record
  Obituaries
  City directories

Solan Family

1.   Patrick (b. Ireland, probably County Galway) m. Mary Lavasse
2.   Thomas [Civil War vet.] (b. ca. 1833, Ireland, d. 1915*, Manchester, NH) m. Ann Lynch (b. ca. 1851, d. 1893*, Manchester)
3.   Elizabeth Ann (b. 1881*, Manchester, d. 1914*) m. Walter F. Hayes [see Hayes Family]

Sources:
  Naturalization Record
  Pension Record
  Obituaries
  City directories

Cass Family

1.   Mother and Father Cass (Warren, VT)
2a. James G. (in 1840 in Warren, Vermont Census) m. Emily A. ____
2b. Martha E. (b. in Granville, VT, d. 1870, Barnard, VT) m. Milton James Allen [see Allen Family]
2c. Emily (b., d) m. Edwin E. Austin [adopted Milton's son Hugh] [see Austin Family]
2d. James E. (b.   , d.   ) m. Ella E. Whitney ca. 1866

Sources:
  1840 Washington County (VT) Census
  Family correspondence

Austin Family

1.   Edwin E. [Civil War vet.] (b., d.), m. Emily Cass
2.   Hugh C. (Allen) (b. 1870, Barnard, VT, d.) m. Kate J. Davis (b., d.) in Boise, ID, 1894
3.   Kathleen E. (b. ca. 1895, Boise, ID)

Sources:
  Wedding notice
  Photos of child

Hatch Family

1.   Edward S. (b., d.) m. Carrie Bell Allen (b. 1867, Barnard, VT, d. ca. 1944, Randolph, VT), 1885 [see Allen Family]
2a. Frank A. [WW I vet.] (b. 1886, d.) m. Florence _____
2b. Leo Adrian Eugene (b. 1899, d.) Randolph m. Emma ____
3a. Ella Mae (b.)
3b. Leah (b.)

Sources:
  Family correspondence
  Photographs

Wylie Family

1. William W., father; Martha Moore Freeman, mother.
2. Lowell M. [WW I vet.] (b. 1891, Eliot, ME, d. 1943, White River Jct., VT) m. Dorothy E. King in Tilton, NH, 1919 [see King Family]
3. Florence M. [adopted by Eugene & Emma King, 1922] (b. 1922, Bristol, NH), m. John W. Bowker in Rutland, VT, 1958 [see Bowker Family]

Sources:
  Photos, state records
  Dept. of Army record

Bowker Family

1. John Wesley m. Julia Bridger Parker
2. John Wesley Jr. [WW II vet.] (b. 1914, Somerset, MA, d. 1996, Somerset, MA) m. Florence M. King, 1958 [see Wylie Family]
3a. Barbara Allen (b. 1958, Brockton, MA)
3b. Nancy Lee (b. 1960, Fall River, MA) m. Thomas J. Moore in Portsmouth, RI, 1986 [see Moore Family]
3c. Janice Wesley (b. 1962, Fall River, MA)
3d. John W. III (b. 1964, Fall River, MA)

Sources:
  Birth certificates
  Licenses

Moore Family

1. Thomas Joseph m. Margaret Furtado
2. Thomas J. Jr. (b. 1957, Portsmouth, RI) m. Nancy Lee Bowker in Portsmouth, RI, 1986 [see Bowker Family]
3a. Jessica Lynn (b. 1992, Newport, RI)
3b. Thomas J. (b. 1994, Newport, RI)

Sources:
  Public records
  Birth certificates

Adams Family

1. Wilson J. m. Bertha Matilda Neilsson
2. Nelson C. (b. 1917, East Hebron, NH) m. Fay Norma King in Bristol, NH, 1946 [see King Family]
3. Gordon Allen (b. 1951, Franklin, NH) m. Shirley Ann Sargent (b. 1956, Franklin, NH) in East Hebron, NH, 1980
4a. Lisa Fay (b. 1980, Franklin, NH)
4b. William Hugh (b. 1983, Franklin, NH)

Sources:
  Public records
  Family correspondence

**Carrie and Eugene (standing),
unidentified woman**

**Huldah Allen, Barnard, VT,
ca. 1865**

**Carrie (seated) with Frank
and Emma, 1880s**

Milton Allen, Barnard, 1860s

"That rascal Rollie" and
friend, Bascom House, 1894

Hugh King, Bristol, NH,
1920s

Bascom House, Bethel, VT, 1890s

Dorothy with Florence, 1922

Lowell Wylie, ca. 1918

Dorothy, 1917

Florence, Rutland, VT, 1950s

Helen, Bristol, 1920s

Richard Hayes, Concord, NH, 1926

Kathryn, Rutland, VT, 1950s

Helen with Kathryn, Concord, NH, 1926

Part II - Emma and Eugene

What Happened After . . .

By 1874 Huldah was probably dead, and Madison a bit later; the dates given in reports vary widely. Milton lived with his two daughters in Barnard. There apparently was steady contact between the Allen and King families, for in 1876 Milton married Alice King, Mary Ann's daughter, and all the Allens moved to New Hampshire. At some point, perhaps the same time or even earlier, the Kings had also moved to New Hampshire. Records and correspondence place them in Franklin Falls and Enfield.

The Connecticut River valley was home to a number of mills. One of them was the Celloway Mill and this is where Milton's daughter Emma Bertha worked for several years. Also working there was Mary Ann's son Eugene and perhaps his brothers, Edward and Thomas. A number of other King cousins also worked there or in other local mills.

Emma Bertha Allen married Eugene King in 1889 and lived in Franklin Falls, New Hampshire. Her sister Carrie Bell had married Edward Hatch in 1885 and moved to West Randolph, Vermont. Milton and Alice had moved to Bethel, Vermont, and resided in the Bascom House, a boarding hotel.

In 1893 Emma's daughter Gladys Mary was born but "failed to thrive" and died in early 1894. Emma was broken up by the death and spent some time recovering in Bethel, Vermont, with Alice King Allen. Eugene and Emma corresponded during this and other separations.

Emma, who at one time told me she had really never wanted to have any children, subsequently had Hugh, born in 1895, Dorothy in 1901, and my mother Helen in 1904.

★　★　★

One thing that has always fascinated me when reading old letters is the wealth of information they gave about the local scenes and language and customs of the times, quite apart from the comings and goings of the writers. Of course, I still wanted to know "What happened then? What happened after?"

Some of these letters will be included in their entirety, and others will be shortened. One of the most interesting writers was Milton Allen. I fervently wish that someone had saved the letters he wrote home to his mother during the Civil War. He volunteered and served in the 10th Vermont Volunteers and was discharged at the end of his first enlistment. He enlisted again, was wounded severely, and was discharged. At some point he was the color bearer — a dangerous job. They say he was in every battle except Gettysburg. Upon his recovery he enlisted for the third time and was wounded again. The war ended before he was completely recovered from that wound, and he was discharged in June of 1865.

He was either exceptionally patriotic or he just liked a good fight. Most of his ancestors had participated in either the Revolution or some of the subsequent — or earlier — wars. Some members of the family spoke of there having been a full-blooded Indian woman in either the Smith or Allen line. I don't have any proof of that except for what my grandmother and others told me, but if you look closely at Milton's photo perhaps you can see some evidence of it.

I should point out that these families were great ones for nicknames or pet names. Alice is sometimes called Allie, Neal or Neally; Emma becomes Emmy, Minie, Sims, Simmy or Birdie; Eugene is Gene, Jin or Jinny. Carrie Bell becomes Tabbie, etc. Takes some getting used to.

The earliest letters are from Mary Ann King to members of her family. Alice and Milton, who married in 1876, are living in Vermont. Alice had been very ill and was discussing coming home to stay with her mother for a while.

Enfield, NH, Sept 2, 1883

Dear Allie

I will write a little. I have not felt very well, the pounding made me feel some badly but they got along well [some people in the house evidently made a lot of noise]. . . . Jinny [Eugene] went to work today, Walter wanted him to work. . . . Had a letter from Nan, she is as well as when I was there. Ira was sick, his face was badly. Frank stayed two weeks with them.

. . . The young ladys gone to Grantham, not quite as noisy.

Enfield, Dec. 6th, 1883

Dear Milton

I got your very good letter. Oh, yes, your kind words do me good. Poor Allie, she is a great suffer & she does overdo & she can't help it, her makeup is so strong. I feel so bad to think she can't get strong but you know, Dear Milton, that anyone wil have sick dayes but she is better when she is with you so she says, and she can come home when Mrs. Osgood comes.

Yes, our stove is nice but it is bad for one that is sick. So noisy & so much to do she gets tired out & I do so

89

pray you will get your Pension. Can make her a good quiet place and you must try and help me take care of Allie, you know all about her. She can come home & stay & then go back to you, I think it will be a good thing. It is only two weeks to Christmas, I guess she can stay until then.

I hope you will get something yourself before long. Have you sent in all things they want. . . . You will have to take Allie across your knee and then she will mind . . . Yes, I hope you will get you a home for you want one as well as Allie does.

Enfield, Dec. 6, 1883

Dear Allie

You will want to here from me by this time. . . Today the boys is skating on the pond. I get along well & want to see you badly but am glad you are in better quarters. Your father let his tong slip, sayed I should think you would be lonesome. I sayed I guess I be but she is got a good still place. I am so glad. Somtimes if I could go out some it would be better. Dont get homesick if you can help it.

Well had some cold day, is very nice today. Johny & I try to take all the comfret we can. He sayes lonesome without Neal [Alice]. Jinny says so to. Well my dear Neal you had a hard time so Milton tells me, yes come home but you can stay till Christmas or two weeks. Milton wants you to & try to have him get you a home so you can go when you want to if he can. I am glad you are a coming but the awfull noise they make I hate to have you bare it.

Oh yes, the farmers think a woman can bair more than a man & the wimmin think so to, but you or I cant with our presant state of health & I am glad Milt is good to you. Hope he will be & you must mind him. Dont work much, do just as he thinkes you ought. Mrs. Osgood can bare more than most. Sick people can live without eating in a low ___ state. She has not been down to our state, she could not live or come home in a month.

Enfield, Dec. 22, 1883

Dear Allie

. . . I want see you but I take comfort thinking you are so much better of. I do not have to hear the stomping guy makes a lot noise with his feet now. The snow has come, good sleighing here & there. Shaker Mill gone on three quarter time so the men go quarter past seven & come out a quarter past four, so you see we have all the good we can.

Your father won't have so much for anyone I suppose. He did not say one word. I think he was glad of it, so far they stay over to run until supper time. . . . I wrote to Carrie to come & spend Christmas but she could not. She sayed the mill stop for 3 weeks, she was doing housework. I wish she could come, she wrote she was agoing to save her money now . . . She is pretty young to work so hard. I am glad she has not to do housework long.

Well I am glad Milton sent his papers, he will know pretty soon what he will have. Hope he will get something. Well dear Neal I go over the same old ground. I do not wash dishes as I did, I could not the cold was too much for me . . . How nice for you to get a still place get rested. I think Mrs. Osgood a brave woman and I hope she will get well. Would not you like to see her.

Dear Milton

Yes dear Milton I am as glad as you be to have Allie
so much better, & yourself I am so glad we are on the mend.
. . I don't wonder you like to tell of Neally. She is quite apt
to do to much but she will mind pretty well. Hard to set and
do not much, can't do it, a person of Allie's makeup.

*Milton was looking for another place where he and Alice could
live. The following tells of his progress.*

Royalton, Vt, Aug. 21, 1886

Dear Allie

Hims is not dead but has been quite sick so much so
that we only this day finished up our hay & grain & today
or this afternoon I have been on the Scout to Bethel, So.
Royalton & Royalton. I can do the best to Bethel at the
Gilson house [Milton says Gilson but it is the Bascom
House]. He will keep us both for 6.00 a week & the room is
better & the more I think of it I think it is the best place
yet. I like the Royalton landlord but it ain't up in stile. Yes,
Allie, my darling, come to Bethel Monday Aug. 23d if
posible cause I have only one week to be off but shall stay
over it a little.

Yes 6.00 for both & a cool quite large room is awful
cheap & they live so we can stand it for it is called better
than the Wilson house. Oh dear, the awful cramp is in my
hand so that I can hardily write but rest will stop that I
trust. But loved one the time seems so short but to be
together all of the time makes it quite a time. Allie will of

course know what to bring, might take a trunk just as well cause we have but a few steps to go to the hotell. Now if you can get this Monday morning all right & good. You could come Monday, oh I so hope you can. Being a registered letter you may be notified. It will come down on the night mail so it will be there Sunday morning.

Oh hope & pray hims wife will be reasonably well when this comes. Well, by by, leave all love & news till have seen my own blessed darling wife. Don't feel bad cause poor hub could not get round before cause he done all he could & live & was so sick & worn when he was bad that he could not really stand.

Hers Hub

Mary Ann's letters to Alice continue:

Dec. 21st, 1886

Tuesday morning & Minny [Emma] washing & Tommy gone to work for Celloway this week . . .

Franklin Falls, Jan 23, 1889

Dear Alie

. . . I get tired some & know you do for there is a good deal to do. I am so glad you are so much better & I am carefull more so than I ever before. I do not work to hard & don't you think I have not got chilled this winter . . . I am so glad you got a person with some feeling.

Gramp had been quite good until this winter . . .

Well, Mrs. Powell is worse, she got well & now she is worse than ever. The Dr told her she had not ought got married. I suppose they could not let well enough alone.

Mr. Stevens was mad, he sayed the cow trobled folks so she got go. He hated to see her go. Gramp wanted what he paid for, she staid six months & no thanks.

Franklin Falls, Feb. 1st, '89

Dear Alie

. . . I am glad Milt did not get hurt any worse. It must feel bad.

. . . We get along well. Gramp moved his bed into the barn. He was quite pleasant some of the time but he get cross. He is now & dear Neally I am glad you been away for you would got tired out last Sunday & many more awful hours. Sunday we was getting along all pleasant, I got him papers to read & all of a sudden got mad because Seth brought us ___ coffee. I told him we all made mistakes . . . You see your being at home does not make any difference.

Feb. 9th, '89

Dear Alie

. . . Hope dear Neal this will find you & Milton well. I have no news to write, but Oh what a terribel accident there has been at the bridge near Woodstock depot. O how teruble, sixty burn and killed a girl from Sharon. I

94

new her father but he was not hurt. Her name was Follet. How sad to think of so many burnt to death.

. . . Well Mr. Dodge has gone on to the ten hours a day law so the hands work ten hours a day. Edward likes that. I am glad & all will in time . . . Next week the Knights of Labor have a fair & dance but B.F. has not ben for a long time. The Ladys came to get us to do something & B.F. wanted we should bake a turkey & I told him we could.

. . . & Milton how is his place, better I hope. Mrs. Powell got better & gone home.

May 1st, 1889

My dear daughter Allie

. . . Well I want you should get me some laudum & get Birtha some of the pepsin. The other kind that she [physician] sent you hurt Minie . . . I had a letter from Aunt Nancy yesterday & she is quite smart, she wrote, better than she ever thought she could be. And Alick come home with his wife & two little girls to stay. The eldest is 4 years old & the other 8 months. She sayed they could not get along any longer alone and she sayed they liked Alicks wife very much. She wanted I should stop [by], she wrote Eilfurd moved of of the hill most to the village & I could stay to Mary Ann, they got a plenty of room & she would come to the depot for me. She sayed Mary wanted me to come but I do not know as I can for I do not know as I shall be well enought.

Nancy sayed Chrit had got so he speakes to Ira & ask him to ride with him 3 times, I am so glad. How bad it is to not speak to a sister, one that done so much & as poor Aunt Nancy has done.

Well B.F. just come in to dinner & he sayed he got a job sorting. Parson came & told him he want to give him the job of sorting & Oh I am so glad I do not know what to do,

95

he was shucking around & he was real glad. Now we feel better. Minie was so glad I never saw her show so much gladness . . .

[From what I have read, the use of narcotics such as laudanum was pretty prevalent in these years before the drug laws were passed. Emma told me that someone in the family was a frequent user. It may have been Mary Ann. I don't know if Alice got the habit too, but it may account for her frequent spells of ill health.]

February 2nd, '89

Dear Milton

. . . I am very glad you taken comfret this winter & Alie is so much better for she can get out some & it is so much better for her & I am so glad you did[n't] get hurt any worse. How long shall you stay in Bethel, all of the time. I wish you could get increase of pension, I see a good many men have this last week . . . How do you get along with Mr. Pastock, does he do any better.

Thomas King wrote the following to Alice:

[May 1889]

Dear Ally

We received your letter last night, were glad to hear that you were coming soon. Gammer says that she will be very very glad to have you come home, so will we all. Gammer has had another sick turn . . . Was quite smart Wednesday but she had a lame side and the worryment and work caused her to overdo . . . Have news that Gramp is wool sorting, began work Thurs.

The Hon Geo. W. Nesmith is dead, heart failure. Judge Nesmith was born Oct. 23, 1800. . . Business is better here now. Are building the rails . . . Well, good by for this time, are lotting on your coming. Will ride in a cart and have your pickture took. Hope Milton will have a big pension soon. I guess that he will soon when the pension officers get to his case.

Mary Ann died in 1890. Emma and Eugene had married in 1889 and both were still working in the mills when they could get work. They were living in Franklin Falls, New Hampshire. They addressed Alice and Milton as mother and daddy.

June 6, 1891

My dear little muzzer [Alice]

Guess you wonder if we are all died on the farm. Guess not, muchly all alive and kicking like h-ll to get the crops hoed.

. . . We have papered 1 bedroom and the kitchen looks better sold 6 1/2 dozen eggs, spect the cow now soonly, don't know for sure but think shall get her.

It rained so hard all decoration day we could not go. It seemed bad not to but a ___ me to so I should had to stay at home anyway. It went 8 weeks this time, I got to nervous for fear we should not come to the farm I guess, but I feel better now. Will proceed to get fat, my Dimmie [Eugene] weighs 135 2 weeks ago. Think more now it seems funny to have him feel so good. He will get out in the yard and run and say farming is a bugger. He got pretty tired last night, hoed corn all day, but he said it was a good tired not completely exhausted. You ought to see him with his boots on and a week's whiskers on his face.

Chicken and Rooster

Wednesday [1891-92]

Dear mother

On High St. & we are all as well as usual except I have got a hard cold. How are you & Billdad [Milton] this awful cold weather. It was 11 above zero this morn, as cold a night as we have had this winter. Birdie [Emma] is feeling good, the best I have ever seen her.

Well it will soon be spring again & we shall have to begin to think of farming on the old homestead & planting ginseng in the swamp & other things to many to think of tonight.

The cow & calf are doing well. George Hunt takes care of them, the heffer is a good one, looks just like Grafton, same collor. . . Should like to go hornspouting up at Crosses with Milt again.

Gene

Benjamin King writes to his daughter:

Franklin Falls, Jan 17th, 1892

Dear daughter

I got a letter from you the other day and was glad to hear from you. Was glad to hear that you are well at the

98

present time. Thomas and myself are keeping house, we got sick of boarding houses so we are trying to keep house. We have got a nice house and are living like Kings. Thomas does the most of the work and I do the marketing and we get along first rate. We have a nice house and we have a nice room for you when you come down to see us.

We are hoping that you can come and see us soon. I am working in the Stevens mill at present shearing. Eugene and Minie live very near us in an upstairs tenement very much alike ours. We hope that you can stop with us the most of the time . . . We have a father in the house [cat], Maltese and white toes, goatee under his chin and five toes on each fore foot.

Come down as soon as you can. My health is poor this winter. My breathing troubles me this winter and my heart is becomeing very irregular and I have got to be almost a skeleton, and besides I am seventy years old so you see my race is nearly run. I feel this winter that I shall soon join the gammer. Do not be alarmed at this despondent tone as may feel better soon. The fact is I am feeling better since we commenced housekeeping.

Write often and we will try and answer your letters. Tell us in your next letters when you are comeing to see us. My respects to Milton and tell him to come when he can.

Yours truly B. F. King

Am not certain who is the Aunt Clara who penned the following letter to Alice, but it contains observations about two items of interest: Halley's Comet, and the Lizzie Borden case. I cannot identify the William referred to here. He may or may not have been a Cass:

White River Junction, VT Dec 7th, 1892

Dear Niece

   . . . Well the comet did not hit the old Earth this time. Lizzie Borden will have to swing. The grand jury knew what they were about.

   Next Saturday there will be a supper at Mrs. Wheeler's . . . I shall not go I have just heard that Brother William's wife is dead, no particulars.

                      Your aff. Aunt Clara

Several members of the Cass family write to Emma at various times. I have trouble keeping these Casses straight:

                   Rochester, VT May 7th 1893

Dear Emma & husband

   . . . Clara had a letter from Carrie and she said you were sick. Are you better and what has been the matter. Carrie said she should be so glad when warm weather ever comes and I guess we all shall. Such a hard rain storm as we have had this last week. The river has been very high and done lots of damage all around us. There was a fearful wind here some weeks ago. My father had a barn blown down and a long shed killed his sheep and hurt a cow so she had to be killed. Our folks never went to bed all night.

   Had a letter from Aunt Ella last week. She said one man over in Lincoln had 20 cows killed at the same time.

   . . . Clara has been to school 28 weeks, the last 2 weeks she lost on account of having the chicken pox. She had it very hard indeed, her spots are not all gone yet. She will begin to take music lessons next Tuesday, will take a while this summer. She has been out and found a very few mayflowers but she is delighted with those. Has had a very pleasant time all winter going with the young people to school and evening sociables, partys and concerts. Such a tall girl as she is you would hardly know her still she is our "baby."

. . . Had a letter from Mother Cass lately, said she should stay with Mrs. Goldsbury this summer, was very well. Sade wrote they were all very busy with them in their ditches. Hugh and Harry both owe Clara letters. He wrote Carrie that they did not know that he knew who he was. Aunt Ella said Uncle Jim was road commissioner there, soon would start the road machine.

Hugh, who was adopted by Emily Cass Austin and her husband Edwin, wrote to Emma from Idaho:

Garden Valley, Idaho, May 25 '93

Dear Sister

As it has been a long time since I received your last letter I will now do so. I have moved since I last heard from you. I am now working in a saw mill for a mining co. in the snow. I do not know how long I shall stay here or where I shall go next. Times are very dull in Idaho this summer and money is scarce here now. I think I may go to california in harvest if things do not go better than now. If the Chinese have to go it will be a fine country for a working man. There is always plenty of work on the fruit ranches there. If the Chinaman would go wages would be better.

I had a letter from Aunt Ella [Mrs. James E.] the

other day. She thinks that I am coming east this fall but I don't know when I shall come, but I hope that I may some day see my sisters. So goodby.

Hugh

Alice Allen kept up quite a correspondence with Emma and Eugene:

Bascom House, Bethel, VT May 30, 1893

I will begin my letter so I can finish in the morning for I said I would write Wed & MJ has got tickets for the play and I may not feel just like writing in the morning. I went to the services this afternoon. Address by the Rev. Walter Dole and a good one too. They had a base ball game that most all went to and it just spoiled the spirit of the day for all thoughts were on that and just as they all got there there was an awful hard shower and all got soaking wet and it served them right every one said. The GAR boys were all glad. All the good'uns were in the Hall and did not get wet.

Oscar Campbell came down and stayed to dinner with us. His pension is 22 dollars a month. Your daddy looked nice all dressed up today, but he lookd slim and poor in health. In fact he looks worse than he is for he is better than when I went away and his cold is most gone. He was at the depot and awful glad to see me. He is going to rest up this week and I think rest would do him more good than medicine, and he says he is going to come down when I do or shortly after and have a month to scout around and rent. He has got in the Beehive Bank 7.00 dollar registered all in ten ct pieces. I think he has done well. He feels awful sorry to not go haying but of course don't see as anything better

102

could be done. I am all safe had no adventurs, only one man wanted I should use his mileage. Said I would save 25 cts. The cars filed up at the Junction with people starting for the Worlds Fair [Chicago]. I was glad I had not got to ride way out there, I had enough as it was.

Oh now I will tell you what daddy bought that he felt sick over. It was an emery wheel that you can run with your foot and grind knives and scissors and anything. You never saw so cheap a looking box in your life. I wish you could have seen him when I asked him what it was he bought. Oh his mouth, Simmy [Emma] knows how he looks. Well he brought it out and adjusted it on the stand and I told him it was splendid, we could grind anything and he felt better. A man had it and talked about how nice it was and he guilty then wanted to kick himself as I did when I got the corset.

Poor Mrs. Rood has come to grief. The man that lives in the same house was kicked by a horse in his stomach last Sunday and was brought home. He had fainted and they thought him dead and it frightened Mrs. Rood so she had stroke of paralysis so her mouth is all drawed out of shape and she cannot use her left arm or side, and they say the man cannot live.

Wednesday morn

We had a splendid show. Their new scenery is grand and the new Hall was packed from floor to balcony. There must have been a thousand people there and they had sold tickets enough to come to 170 dollars yesterday and there were lots more come. I wanted chicken and her rooster to be there. How does chicken feel this day. Did you go anywhere yesterday. The Bristolers will have a nice day and Gyppy will be glad to see her old manse.

Rolly is going to Chicago a week from Tuesday.

103

Chicken ought to have seen him last night dressed up in his nice black full dress suit and diamond pin. He looked so tweet.

Bascom House, June 11, 1893

We have just been to tea and your dad has gone to do chores and owing to a severe thundershower he has had to change his togs. There has been 3 heavy showers thunder and lightning to match. He is feeling lots better. His stomach is better and he says he feels almost well. He has been resting for 3 days. He and Mr. Pierce went up in the woods one day. He got a little ginsing one big root but there is none to be had anywhere around this place, it's been so gone over.

Rolly has gone to the worlds fair and Ephream Wester went with him. I wish the highwayman would get hold of them and scare the life out of them.

June 18th 1893

My Darling Chicken

Thanks for your letter that came this morning. Your dad had it in his "packetts" & came near forgetting to give it to me but I was on the lookout and captured it. He has gone on a jinseng bout . . .

Mr. and Mrs. Black have gone to Boston for a week. I have trained her so she don't bother me at all. I took your way and wouldn't go to see her unless I was a mind to and she don't light on me ever time I go by the door. We have another sick lady in Mrs. Brown's room. Her hair is just like

104

yours, she can't be more than 22 or 3 and she has the consumption and such a hollow cough. She came from West Hartford & knows Sam Bruce & Bell. She says Bell is a nice woman and her husband is conductor on the way freight. I pity her so I don't know what to do. His Nibs is trying his best to cure her but he cannot.

   . . . Well your daddy has got back at 5.30 and is going to dress up for supper. He got about a pound of shang and he did not go very far.

In the following, Alice makes oblique reference to an impending event in Emma's life:

June 19, '93

   . . . Does it bother you to do your work and do you heave up Jonah as much as you did. What did Eva say to your change of girth.

   . . . I have not heard from Carrie but we are going up there I think next Saturday night on the 5. Your Pa wants to go and see a piece of woods up that way.

   The other noon as we went down to dinner there was a boy 12 years old gave a note to your Pa and it was from Inez Campbell French and it was her boy. They came from Dacotah last week. She is up to Roswell Morgan's and I expect she will be down here.

Mother

105

Another letter from Hugh Austin:

Garden Valley, Idaho July 2, '93

Dear Sister Emma

As I wrote you some time ago and have got no answer yet I think I will write again. I have moved from Boise Valley to Garden Valley up in the mountains where it is cool and pleasant. I am now working in a saw mill. I am Ratchet setter for which I get the large amount of fifty dollars a month and board. I did work in the mines awhile but I got promoted to work in the mill for the same company.

Things will be very dull here the Fourth as we are thirty miles up in the Sawtooth mountains and no place to go and celebrate, so I guess we will have to go hunting or fishing. There are lots of deer and salmon and trout here and some bear. One came into camp and killed our hog the other night so we out to have him to be eaten.

I heard from Carrie the other day but have not heard from father for a long time and I wrote to him last so I guess I will wait a while longer and see what is the matter.

Ella Cass married Martha Cass's brother James E. Cass:

Warren, VT Sept 5th 1893

Dear Emma

. . . Each day has brought its labor, and demands upon my time so that my correspondents have all been

106

neglected, or rather, all save Hugh. I do not allow myself to put aside writing to him. For somehow it seems as though he belonged to me. At least, he has taken the place in my affections of my own little boy I lost so many years ago.

How do the days find you and yours now? Well I hope. I was pleased to hear the bit of news you wrote me in your last. It will be another bond to strengthen the love between yourself & husband. Your home will be all the more pleasant for its coming. And may it prove a sunbeam in infancy and childhood, and a comfort and blessing in later years.

I had a letter from Carrie a short time ago with an invitation to attend little Frank's seventh birthday party. Had to decline the invitation as it was not convenient for poor Uncle to leave at that time. I intend to visit her the last of this month if possible.

Received a letter from Hugh about a week ago. He was well and working rather hard I should think from what he wrote.

Have the rainstorms done any damage to you lately? The river here has not been so high since the big freshet in '68. It carried of one mill and machinery, and the highways are badly washed. James says it will cost $200.00 to put them in as good condition as before the storm.

The clock is striking nine and I must close. Now take the best of care of yourself now, and during your confinement so that there may be no unfavorable results from it.

Auntie Ella Cass

Emma's sister Carrie Bell writes to her:

My dear sister

    . . . I expect by this time your family is larger. I hope so for your sake. How is mama, well I hope.

    The wind blows awful hard today and tonight I think it blows worse so is awful lonsome, the leaves falling all around. I wish it could be always summer don't you, or do you like the winter best. I think Ed does, he seems to feel better in cold weather. And has Gene gone back in the mill yet. It is hard dull times all round. I guess Ed is in luck this time, he has a good job in Man's livery stable for all winter.

    We went to Tunbridge fair last Wednesday, had a good time. Should have a better time but I worked to hard and got so tired I was almost sick, and then the Smith Block just across the road from us caught a fire a little while after we started. They telefoned to Tunbridge so we herd in about a hour after we got on the ground.

    You can guess I've felt as though we should like to be at home but I was later to think of it we could not get back in time to save anything if our house caught. The fire company put it out after a while, lot of damage done we think. We have got a firebug among us somewhere here. Got a NY detective hunting for him. Have had lots of fires all round us. I tell you we jump when that old fire bell rings.

Your sister Carrie

The Bristolers, Adelaide Victoria Huntoon King and Edward F. King, send their congratulations to Eugene:

Bristol, Nov. 2, 1893

Dear Gene

We were much pleased at the news and hope they will both do well. Tell Berth she has done nobly, we didn't want a boy. Shall be over to see our Niece as soon as we think she has acquired company manners so she would enjoy the visit.

Is your heart set on the name. Grammy didn't like the Gladys. Hope you have not fully decided on it. Haven't any more time now, have to work all day. Love to you all and let us know if things don't get along.

Addie King

Carrie Hatch writes to Alice:

West Randolph, Nov. 8, 1893

Dear mama

Your long looked for letter received and I am so glad for Emma all though she probly wanted a boy. Tell her when I have my next boy I will swap with her. Ed's sister Mrs. Fish met with a mishap Monday and lost hers. She feels bad about it and I am afraid she is not going to get right up.

Uncle Jim and Aunt Ella Cass came over last week and made me a visit. Stay two nights, had a grand visit. Have not herd from Hugh since I wrote you last. Uncle Will has moved down to her father's, Morris. Don't think her father will live a great while.

What are you going to name the baby, and who is going to name it . . . I suppose Emmy sits up by this time. How does she like tending baby. I think it is fun if one has not got a lot of work to do. I always had so much to do when Frank was a babie to enjoy it as much as I should again if I had the chance than if it is always in the way.

Do you hear from Hugh, I wonder if he will really come east or will he back out. I wish he would come, does he ever say anything to Emmy about being married. He told me he thought I missed it, said there was lot more fun being single and independent.

Tabbie

Emily Cass sends postcard to Emma:

Rochester, VT, Nov. 19th, 1893

Dear Emma

We were delighted to hear the fine news and glad you all are comfortable. Think the name fine, tell her to be a "good girl" and wife. Stayed here all night two weeks ago last night. Both well and Mother Cass has been here with us a week now, gone to Warren is quite smart. We have sold our home at the village and came down on to father's farm to care for them the rest of their days. Father is very feeble with heart disease and mother quite poorly. My sister pretty well. Clara has to be carried to school, we are 2 miles below the village.

Send me a card so I may know how you are get along.

E. A. Cass.

Ella Cass conveys congratulations to Emma:

Warren, VT Nov. 20, 1893

Dear Emma

Accept congratulations from your Uncle and Auntie on the birth of your daughter. May she prove a comfort or blessing to you now and for all time. I think you have selected a very pretty name for her. If I were to suggest any change, it would be that you might call the middle name Martha instead of Mary, for your own Mama.

I had felt confident that when the little one came it would be a boy, and I was going to propose that you call it Hugh. But it is the unexpected things which happen.

. . . Grandma Cass is with me now so I'll not have to stay alone while he is gone . . . I am so glad to think that Hugh is coming East and hope if he comes he will never regret it. Of course it will seem very different to him here, not so much for excitement. But do not believe he will ever be sorry for coming.

I shall have to close now for I want to write to Hugh tonight. Take good care of Emma and the little one and write to your Auntie when convenient, she is always glad to hear from you.

Your Auntie Ella Cass

Another letter to Emma from brother Hugh:

My Dear Sister

As it has been some time since I have heard from you
I think it is time I was doing it. I am now in Boise again, do
not know how long I will stay here or what I will do. Times
are very dull here now and will be until spring. I have not
heard from father since last spring so I do not know
anything about him, but his wife wrote to me some time ago
and I am going to answer it today. I was surprised to hear
from her but was glad to hear from her. Think by the letter
she writes she is a very nice woman and would be easy to get
along with as a step mother. How old is she and what kind
of a looking woman is she.

It has been raining here for nearly two weeks and do
not know when it will stop, so I guess winter is here at last
and for all time.

There is to be a Firemans Ball at the Hall tomorrow
night and I am going to attend and do some dancing myself.
I have a very pretty girl, her name is Kate Davis. She is a fair
haired thing and weighs one hundred and eighty pounds so
we get along fine. She is what brought me back to Idaho
from Calif. and if it was not for her I would say good bye to
Idaho tomorrow. Now write soon.

From Hugh

112

Alice gives a hint of things going not so well:

Bethel, VT,   Dec. 12th, 1893

Dear Emmy

. . . How I want to see little Private Umpson [Gladys], little dove, is she better. Strange her food does not seem to do her any more good. How would it do to write to His Nibbs Dolliver & Co. & tell her case as near as can be & await results. If she is sick you must let me know.

. . . Are you feeling well as you did. Miss Childs said for anyone as sick as you to do their work in 5 weeks was going better than most of folks. I just hear Rolly coming for the new schoolmarm. He is going to take her to the show. He has bought his mother a new crimson velvet sofa, a beautiful thing. Such is life, some have money & some don't. Well, he don't have to work much like poor Private Umpson. I would like to see him spin in Stevens mill. He wants to buy his mother a diamond ring but she says she won't wear it if he does.

Milton brings Gene up to date Bethel-wise:

Bascom House, Dec. 13, 1893

Tuesday eve at Bascom and the 2 occupants of Room No. 10 are writing to their children & will say to Genie & Simmey that it is a bleak cold night for a that. The Opera

House is fast filling up to see the Great Play of Little Lord
Fauntleroy, but the little Mother & the Billdad did not want
any of it on their plate cause why, we went last night to see
the Village Vagabond played & it was very good but the
same little kidd that is to be the little lord tonight had an
active part & we got all of his prattle we cared for. So we are
to wait for more mascaline tradgedy to be on the docket.

Well chilluns our wood here now happens to be 4
foot so it takes me just about all of the time & a little more
to keep the some over 20 stoves red hot at Bascom & the
Cashiers work to see to for all anything else. So you see I am
in no shape to get lazy & I have 3 cords 4 foot coarse wood
for chuncks to saw to Sylvesters & I have commenced to go
on to roofs to clear gutters & get off snow and lots of saw
fileing. If I had a place & everything needed I could vary
near get steady work fileing. But it don't come right so I do
not do any more of it than can help. Billdad thinks we will
have lots of snow before it is time for jensing to grow again
which I am very ancious to have get a early start. Shall never
give it up Gene but what the root is agoing to be the corner
stone to our Prosperity.

Allie has come back much better than I expected. She
has gone into the work like a heroine in a book. Mended me
all up so quick & I was all to tatters & shreds.

The Grandma has to worrey considerable about all
the kidds at Franklin. If the little one can stand the food
untill it gets older it will be all right I think & hope, and if
Gene & Sims get on to the farm I know they will be & it
must be for the mill life will kill in time. It don't & cannot
agree with anyone to be shut up. Yes, I am certainly better
now but the old crop ain't all well yet cause it growls &
burns at times but I think it will all get right again in time. I
think such cold weather & air is bad for me.

There is not much going on up this way only traid &
teaming lumber & bark is coming in big. The more I have

thought of Enfield the more I want to hunt it over some now that country we went over the Sunday we all went to the Side Slide. Jensing is a native of granite soil & there was nothing but granite out there. Probiley no one has got on to it there, we must have a scout there another summer shure.

I have got us a backwoods revolver, a long heavy one 32 center fire self cocking or the old way as you wish. Poor A ain't quite stout enough in her hands to work it good, with that one need not fear to meet a panther or anything else. It will shoot 20 round in good shape so you see if we should camp out we can, armed and all ready to be let alone & allowed to hunt our roots in peace.

Now there is some knives over to Tuppers that I will get us one & we can skin bears or cut sled stakes. They are awfull handy to have to trim trees with birches etc., etc. If we have a big berry year the next & we are in shape to tend to them I will contract them up here for 15 per quart & we will help make a payment that way or quite. Oh you know Sims & I was talking about her planting some jenseng seeds in some of her boxes so to see how long it would take them to sprout or come up. I wish Simmy would & if there were no seed left will send some, will put some in letter anyway for I think where it was warm it would not take long.

Horses are being almost given away up here, real good kind workers & good on the road. There was 4 sold at auction one for 13.00, the others 20 to 25, never knew them to be so cheap, hope it will last.

We will see if we can't get a start next summer or know the reason we can't.

More letters from Alice:

Dear Jin & Berth

. . . It has been some time since I got your letter & I
wonder how Private Umpson is getting along. Mrs. Osgood
has come & got the room old lady Brown had last winter &
Mrs. Coleman [school teacher] has the one opposite & Mrs.
Slack is away for the winter so I have quite pleasant
neighbors.

Nellie Osgood wants to know all about Gladys & I
told her how she cried & did not gain & we gave her
Mell___ food & she said she did not think much of it for
when Gail was a kid he was poor & everything she gave him
did not agree with his stomach until she tried Ridges food,
and in a month he had gained so you would not have known
him & she gave it to Burns & he never was sick. She says it
makes them sleepy & seems to help the colic. She said she
tried everything & no good till she got the Ridges food.
(Ridges food brought Gail Osgood from a sick squaling kid
to a fat healthy one.)

You know it is what Gamma had & you might try
it. She said she thinks she did not make it so rich as the
directions say. Mrs. Carl Cushman has only given her baby
girl cold milk & she is so fat she cannot put her little hands
together. She would not drink the milk warm, would spit it
out but cold was allright.

Wish we could find out just the right thing for her
stomach. Did Dr. Drake think she was healthy & her
stomach right. You must all be careful & not get the grippe.

[probably sent to Gene]

I got your letter tonight & was glad to hear from you. Gladys got some nice presents. Glad she has a bed, she seems to have everything done for her, strange she don't get over the colic but there is something that makes it. Others claim to have them cry & do just so & have found the right thing at last so they develope into fat kids that don't cry. Seems as tho she must be better to gain a pound in a week. Yes, Berth must have her hands full, will she let any of you fellows help any. Seems as tho you might mop on Sunday & get the washing done & let Jack get supper & wash the dishes. Never mind if everything ain't just so spotless & in order and clean.

I would like to come right down & help the girl, I would start today. And the old boy says I may before long. And now I want to tell you, if she is any worse you let us know & I will come at once, but if you could get along a couple of weeks till I get him mended up I will come. You know how he is, if you should write the kid is awful sick he would want me to go & bad as any one, but when she is ailing he thinks I must wait awhile.

I am affraid the girl will get sick, she must let all of you help her if they will. Each one chip a little & the washing would not cost much . . . Now don't take the way I write that I don't want to come for I love to take care of Private Umpson, it's the old boy . . .

117

Milton to Gene & Emma:

Gene & Simmey

　　Your poor old Billdad is down in the office & it is 5
minuits of 4 in the morning of the 1st of February. I am
doing this so the mother dear can sleep. The way of it is
your dad has got pickeled. I probily have a very severe attack
of La Grippe for the first time. I was all right up to the time
of my watching with Mr. Sylvester, feeling so bad & the big
snow storm coming & I had to go on to the Wilson Block.
The wind blew terribly & the snow struck. So it was a hard
job & my throat had commenced to be sore then & my
bones & mussels were acheing hard & up to now it has been
a continuance of the same. Oh children, your old cuss of a
dad cannot remember of ever haveing such a right out & out
sore throat. It just takes hold to swallow, but I think it will
went off in a few days. The mother had not dast to come
untill we know how it is agoing to hang on.

　　Now for a piece of good news. The chances now are
that the poor old Myrick cashier will come out of it. We
have lots of times of giving him up but he has got so he can
eat some considerable. The hickups are playing out so you
see if he only can get something into his stomach he will get
right up. I believe I had my throat once in the Army as sore
as it is now. It was just old terrible & if my throat would let
up now I don't believe I should be so very played out. Allie
wanted I should write a line or to so you could know. Just
the cursed luck, but I have been so sleepy I have not been
able to half write.

　　We have quite a lot of snow this time. We want the
children to write as soon as you get this so we may know

118

just how Simmie & the high private in the rear bunk is, the poor little thing, if Gladys feels like I do it would be all day with her. Now write just as quick as possible.

Alice appends a bit to Milton's letter:

Thursday morning

We are out of paper so I will write a line on him Bildad letter. Your old mother is just wild these days for she knows just how bad her chicken needs her & worrying about Private Umpson. When I wrote that I would come everything was all right & your dad had been so well all winter & now he is having a time of it. Commenced Tuesday, but yesterday was the worst day for this morning he was better, that is he did not ache so bad. I do not think he will be sick long & I will come as soon as he is better, but I wanted to come & take care of the private & help chicken. Write & let me know how you both do. How does she act nights & do you think she is going to get smart. She is 3 months old, quite a kid. Mr. Sylvester is better, it used your dad all up thinking he was going to die.

Now write or have Gene so I can know how everything is for it makes me so nervous to think I can't go & help chicken but it will not be long if he keeps getting better (your dad I mean) before I can come.

Mother

The worst happens. Emily Cass to Emma:

Rochester, VT, April 15, 1894

My Dear Emma

I went with one of our neighbors to the village and got your letter myself. Just as soon as I saw it was from you I feared something ailed the baby. I feared she was dead and I opened the letter and found it was all to true. You both have our whole sympathy for she was a great loss to you all and such a little fellow. How still the house will be and everything you see of hers will make you feel all the worse. But we have to make the best of such affliction for it comes to everyone sooner or later, but as you say it don't make it any easier to bear. I am very sorry she could not live. How long was she sick.

There is a little Nellie Burns 4 months old only second neighbor from us, she is bright as you can think. How they would feel to lose her. I am so thankful your ma could be with you. Wish we could have been near to go and see you but one cannot live near all their friends. Has Carrie gone to see you. I hope she has.

Father is no better any time. I think it is old age with him a very slow going down . . . Still he could hardly walk at all. Will has to draw him in his chair to his room at night, sits up about half the time. Mother still has those bad spells and everyone leaves her weaker, some days cannot walk around hardly any. Affects her to read or sew. Worse, all kinds of food hurt her.

Clara is not in school this spring, I felt that I needed her at home the most. Will has a fine sugar orchard but nothing to do with no house nor tools to work with, everything so run down. He has all his wood split, apple trees all trimmed and the brush burned and now has a hired man to help draw stone for the barn wall. Has not been warm enough to have the workman in it to work yet.

. . . Clara hears from Hugh quite often, has sent her two pictures of his since Xmas. I don't know whether to even think he will come here or not. . . . Now Emma, I wish I could see and visit with you but rest assured I think of you so often in your sorrow. we ought to think Gladys is with the angels which I think she is . . . I hope it will not make you both sick. I hope some time you will come to see us again. Had you ever had the baby's picture taken. I hope so, my brother died when 9 years old and we had no picture of him. All send love.

Ever your Aunt Em

Ella Cass writes:

Warren, VT   April 20th 1894

My Dear Emma

I was pleased to hear from you once more, but deeply grieved at the sad news your letter contained. You have my deepest sympathy in your bereavement. I know what your sorrow is for I have been placed right there myself.

I know that the days will seem long and lonely, but Emma time will heal your grief and the memory of your little one will be like a gleam of sunshine—a golden link forged in the chain that binds our hearts to the more perfect life beyond the "Great Divide." Death is a part of the plan of the universes, and sooner or later comes to us all. I know the going out from our homes of our loved ones seems at first too hard to be borne, and we all are apt to rebel, but if we could only realize that for them 'twas the entrance to a fuller and grander life we might perhaps submit with better graces. We can only wait, and hope, and trust knowing that God in his infinite wisdom and goodness doeth all things well.

Yes, I hear from Hugh quite often. I received one of his photos, the same as he sent to you. I guess there is some determination there. No, I do not think he will ever come east for he is thinking of marrying bye & bye. He says he will send me his ladie's picture before long, that he is getting old and begins to want a home of his own. The lady will not be eighteen for a year so presume he will not be married before that time . . .

from your Auntie Ella Cass

Emma, probably worn out from the baby's illness and death, and working too hard at the mill, has been laid low by a bad cold and is contemplating going up to Bethel for a rest. Alice writes to Gene:

June 1, 1894

Gene

Was awful glad to get your letter . . . You must be awful busy & it does make it hard to have company that talk so much. Did you go to Decoration. We went to the memorial service at the Congo church last Sunday. There were no other churches open that day. Your dad carried the flag with the GAR boys & Sons of Vets. He looked awful nice. All dressed up with white gloves & badges & he looks so much healthier than he did last year. And on Decoration Day they had a fine time . . . They had a splendid address, and a dance at Bascom Hall in the evening.

. . . Everyone wants me to sew for them so I don't get much time. I have earned 2.75 besides I got a new pillow tick & emptied my feathers in that pillow I had up here & made a new cushion from it for my chair & mended for my rooster. He took the mail train for So. Royalton yesterday in the rain (& by the way he has got him a rubber coat). I told him he was not going to get wet this fall. He got a pound of ginseng. It's rained for most 2 weeks.

I can hear the Eddie playing on his cornet. The other night at the dance the man what plays the bass viol played sick so as not to play & took a girl into No. 9 & went to bed. It was not under the stately elms like little Daphne but just as nice for them.

I had a letter from Carrie, she has been sick but she wrote she was coming to see me Saturday. I shall go over to the depot when the mail comes. There is to be a big time here next week. The graduating exercises at the Town Hall & then the Alumni supper at the Bascom House Hall & a band. The Hall will be trimmed & it will be quite a thing.

I am lotting on Emmy's coming up. Wish she could get that cough cured entirely. I think it will do her lots of good to come up. It would be cheaper for her to hire a mileage. I think they can use them on different roads cause May Sanger does. Am glad Gramp got his clothes. Make him go to meeting. Does he still have to change his shirt on Saturday night, too bad.

Milton to Gene & Emma:

June 2, 1894

Gene & Simmey

    The mother bird is reading in bed & it is 10 Friday night but I am agoing to scribble a few lines anyway. Everything is driving at Bethel. The tanery is to rush up a large building to finish leather. It will call for 50 more help & it is hard to get help as there is more work than men & women. They have had to send to the citys to get men & women help in the shoe shop but no matter, I am agoing to hunt the roots about so much if I have to run away in the night. I have ran out 3 or 4 times a little while on Sunday or when it rained great guns. I can find some every time even where I have been before lots of times. Oh I want to get away far enough so to hit where it has not been found & there is plenty of places if one only could make a start.

    Yes, I want to come down so we can take in a circet of 20 milds or so. There is butternuts lots of it in towns ajoining Bristol. I am told that Dorchester had ought to be canvased even if we could find a few places no better than Old Ragged it would help lots. We got 20.00 pretty easy. A fellow at South Royalton went up the Passumsic 20 milds was gone 7 days & got over 200 pounds green. He wants to have me go further on with him. Said he did not go 4 milds from where he went up, but I will write a lot soon & we will see what we can do.

    Maybe the mill will stop a while again but if I could get where it would pay I should want you to come. Confound it, if we had a hundred dollars & did not care & was independent we could go all over Balahack but we haint, but I am going some all the same.

    Good night children dear, do more & better soon.

Emma arrives in Bethel for nearly three weeks' stay; reports to
Gene:

June 6, 1894

Dear Dimie

   Got here all right and got my surprize worked of
good. Mother was sick and did not see me untill she opened
the door and there we stood and looked at each other. She
thought I was Mrs. Safford, left the valice down to the depot.
They was awfully glad to see me. Dadie said it was nice to
come now and then when he got ready to come it not be all
at one time. He says he is coming right after haying and he
thinks that will be all done by the first week in July. So
prepare for a good time and a long hunt for root. In one way
or another he is going to get a list of every kind of root and
bark they use and see if he can't do something besides.
   . . . Did you get drownded out last night. It rained
hard here 5 minutes after I got here . . . Will write soonly
more, don't let Dolly roost on the plants.

Emmy

[Along through here we see a kind of lighthearted teasing: of
Gene by Emma and Alice, of Emma by Eugene. He thinks he is going to
lose her to some other man and she avers that she will not be "mashed"
by anyone. It is all in good fun, although when I first read the letters
(somewhat out of order) it was a bit shocking. They also use some terms
which I'm not familiar with. "Calicoing," for example, is probably their
term for hanky-panky, but I can't be sure about that.]

125

Alice reports to Gene on Emma's arrival:

Gene

Wednesday morning & I have got Emmy. There has
not been a night before since I came here but when I have
looked out when the 5 train went up but last night I was
sick with a puking spell & was on the bed & had locked the
door & someone rapped & I went to the door to tell them I
could not see them & I did not know who it was at first. I
thought it was a Mrs. Safford & I kept waiting for her to
speak & then she smiled & said it's Emmy.

I was awful glad to see her & when daddy came she
was sitting in my chair & he thought first it was a spook. He
was awful glad to see her. I told her if we had Dimmie &
Mike & Possum & Chaky & Dorothy [cats] all would be
nice.

Rolly went to a wedding last evening & he came up
here all dressed in his evening suit & Emmy was awful
mashed & I think he went in & stayed all night with her,
she has the next room. Are you lonesome any, hope not. We
will all be down there by by. Write soon.

Mother

Gene discourses on his bachelor days to Emma. The phrase "to go" shows up in many correspondents' letters. It may have been a private expression:

Darling wife to go

and leave a good man to tend cats. I got your letter last night and was awful glad to hear from you. It seemed a long time since you started, a whole day and a half, only think of it. You must have enjoyed surprising Mother & Milton. To bad mother was sick but it done her good I presume. How do you like it at the hotel. You must look out & not get gone on any men. It is lonesome as the Devel here so still it is not nice a bit but we can stand it thinking that Emmy is having a good time.

We are cat ridden. Betty had a pukeing spell to night. Gramp yelled hey there & I yelled take her out and he took her up and started with her. Was going to leave her in the hall. Says I, don't leave her there to puke on the stairs, put her out, and he started and says gosh Betty was a belching to beat the devil, and I yelled hurry up and fire the cat out doors or she will puke all over the stairs and then she can come in here all cleaned out. Won't need the pan tonight. You see what it is to be cat ridden. Mike caught a robin yesterday. I went out in the shed at noon and both babies had a wing and the shed floor was all feathers and bones & cat turd, looked like slaughter house in hard luck. Those babies are terrors, into everything, I had to fire them tonight.

I hoed some phosphate around the peas tonight, they are growing nice and the potatoes are blossoming. How is that for early potatoes. We are getting along good. Jack is a good boy to work, but I don't like his style of handling house work very well. We have some fun. We got some kerosene in the meat. Gramp said it was the flames flying up around the fry pan. Jack thought a good bit, said nothing but got a little mad and did not build the fire tonight. Was afraid of the oily flames, I suppose, but he got over it pretty soon. I thought he had builded it so I went and made my bed. When I came back there was no fire. Says I, Jack are you going to build the fire tonight, says he, no I guess not I thought you wanted to build it. Says I, no I thought you was going to build it as usual. Says I, I wish when you have such thoughts I wish you would say so and then we should know what to do. Gramp & I just fired the cats, it took us 10 minutes the children are hard to catch as Possum now. They are buggers, they all played in the setting room night before last, was great.

Emma, mother says Rolly staid with you the first night, don't let it happen again. Will forgive you this time. I have had several offers of little girls who say they come and help us out, but I told them that I thought that it would be safer to get along alone untill Emma got back, scared to death of Emma.

The work in the mill is slack as yet, will be for some time yet. The men have gone to bed, I shall go soon. It is lonesome in that big bed all alone. I am afraid some little girl will climb in the bay window and fondle him and then should lose Emma, ah pleasea let Emma man alone. I hope mother wil keep an eye on Emma and see that she does no calicoing as I have no means of knowing what Emma is doing. Hope she will be truener but if she don't it will be just dood again soon. It is still here tonight to have Emma gone and got those children fired.

Jinny

Dear mother

Keep your eye on Emma, she is untruener to her husband so you say. Was not you glad to see the brave girl so soon. What did Milt think when he came in. Oh yes, you said in your last letter he thought it was a spook.

To bad you was sick. We had an arguement on that subject this noon. Gramp said it was to bad you was sick it kinder dampened the ardor, and Jack said he thought it was bad for you to. We said we had no doubt but it was bad all around the board.

You should see your babies, they need basting bad. Possum has no control over them at all. Well, the curfew has just rung so must go in my bed. Well goodby, write as often as you can.

Jinny

Alice checks in again with Gene:

Sunday afternoon, June 10, 1894

Dear Son Jin

It is very hot this afternoon & Emmy and I have been reading some books we got over to Martin's store. I have been asleep this forenoon. We went to church & heard our new Rector, and there was communion service. We are having a splendid time. Emmy is getting rested & don't cough as much & I am going to take her to Dr. Childs & see if she can not be made to feel better. Friday evening we went over to the graduating exercises & we have walked out & sewed & read & eat. This week we will go up to see Carrie.

I hope you can get along good with the housekeeping so she will not have to hurry home. I know you must be awful lonesome but you have the babies & Possom & Big Mike . . . We saw some nice cats into Martin's store where we got the books. The mother had six toes & 2 kittens the same. They looked like Gabey & Dolly.

Will has gone jinseng hunting today. He will come down that way by & by so you can go meet him. Well, get along as well as you can. I know you must miss the girl, she is brave & smart & the men are all wild about her.

Emma to Eugene:

Sunday 4 o'clock, June 10, 1894

Dear Manerkin

We got your nice letter yesterday. Was very glad to hear from you and know you was getting pretty good. Is it really nicer with Emmy there. Mrs. Gilson just the same as told me I could have work here any time I said, so guess I shall stay if the mill work is no good. Is there any more pieces than they was. Mama and me are going up to Carrie's Tuesday and papa and mama are going to Roswell Morgan's the last of the week. We have done quite a lot of sewing, we could have all the work we could do at that place too.

You poor little lonesome husband. Emmy loves you a great big lot better than any one else and all ways will, so don't think I shall like anyone up here better they ain't pretty a bit. [Eugene comments: Tain't so, she loves Rolly & Eddie.] Mrs. Lafond said she heard the mill was going to shut down, have you heard anything of it.

. . . Am glad you set out my plants. I want my

130

rooster, shan't go and leave him again never, pretty lonesome in the dark . . . Dadie is going to haying next week I guess. It is awfully dirty here now the roads got dry. We went to the graduating exercises in the town hall, rather dull. Did not speak so you could hear them at all hardly. Not much fun, got our hats knocked off, and fun generally.

Did you lick Mike for catching robbin. Hope you did. One here has got her nest right under the piazza roof, brings great worms to them, keeps them busy all the time.

When do you want me to come back or had you rather me stay here. Tell me next time you write which will be soon. Popie, do you have to work just as hard as ever. Does Smith say anything about my coming back. Am having an awfully good time, got weighed in the depot 127 as usual, 142 by an by maybe.

Gene to Emma:

June 12, 1894

My darling little bride
　　of 5 years standing . . . My work is about the same, there is no more work on your job than there was but I guess there will be in a few weeks. Mrs. Estray has been out sick, calicoed I guess. We are getting along pretty good of course. It is not so nice as it is to have our bridekin to care for you but can stand it for a while. Am awful glad to hear you are feeling better, stay just as long as you want to Birdie, get good and rested. We can get along. It does me lots of good to know you are haveing a good time and feeling better. Don't worry about us, we are all right so far. You had better see Dr. Childs, perhaps, as she can help you to get

well again. How is mother & Milton. It has been 90 deg. in the shade for 2 days, makes the corn grow.

Write soon, bring down 4 or five dogs when you come to eat up our scraps. We hate to throw anything away. Hoed your & Ma's sweet peas tonight, the garden is looking fine. The cucumbers have reached the top of the box. Write soon, I have to get some more papper and envelops before I can write again, am all out but this half sheet.

My dear wife, it is cooler today and seems good. There is no news to write about. It is the month of roses and they blossoming here. Have you made any mashes or seen anyone you could love better. Shall have eggs for dinner. Want to see Emma & mother & Milton & talk it over, shall soon I suppose. Shall have to close, love to all.

Jinny

Emma writes from her sister's home. The "cashim" she mentions is money, her and Gene's word for it.:

West Randolph, VT, June 13, 1894

My own dear husband to go

How do you get along this lovely morning. I got your nice letter and cashim yesterday morning. Papa brought it up when he come. Mama and I come up to Carrie's Tuesday morning. I think soon she will come down with me, she and Frank. He is a smart kid you will have lots of fun with him. Am glad the garden is growing so good, and the cats are all right. I think any way I shall come back next Friday, that is the 22, if you can get along another week. I am feeling a good deal better. Ms Childs has give me some medie. One kind makes my head ache so I can't take that.

Does Smith say anything about me. Do the pieces begin to pile up any yet or is the whole thing going to stop, do you think. Wish I knew for sure. Oh dear, how I want to see you, it seems like 10 years. Wish you could come up, it is so pretty here. Everything is so green. Carrie has a pretty place, 5 rooms right downstairs, or 3 down 2 up, $6 rent right on the main streets and lots more to rent.

I wish you would go to Myra's and get your meals till I come home, and then it would not matter how they washed the dishes. You could sleep to home of _____, anyway get your dinner and supper there. Please, I should feel better about you.

Will write good long letter somday. Did you go to Hill yet.

Emmy wife

[When I read this series of letters, I have to laugh at those current know-it-alls who proclaim that "women didn't work outside the home in the 19th century." Women worked—in droves. All along the Connecticut River valley thousands of women worked— and not all because they had to. Many of them worked because they wanted to. Later on, when the mills either closed or curtailed their operations, the women were forced back into their homes—there to rely on a man's wages.]

Thursday eve, June 14, 1894

My dear wife

I received your nice letter and was glad to know you was haveing so good a time & feeling better. You no need to feel worred about me, I am all right. You never knew a King to suffer much. I am cure of the buggers. Jack washes the dishes better now so I guess we can stand it a week longer.

The pieces do not get ahead any yet, there is not enough for those girls they got, I presume they will be more soon. It is to bad that Carrie is sick, it would do her good to come down & make us a visit and get rested. It is awful still down here without Emma. But have Dolly & Shakey & Pot & Mike left, you can bet it makes it interesting at meal times. I boiled some veal for them tonight, they like it.

Oh, Berth, Supt. Danniell stoped me and said when is your wife coming back. I said I got a letter 2 days ago saying she wanted to stay 2 weeks longer. He says, Oh, I thought she was coming back right off, I want her to run our new Mayo Creaser machines. Says if she will come I will pay her fair back. Says I, don't think she could run them on account of her health. Says I, she has tried it twice and it made her sick. Says he, she can do this if she can stand on her feet at all, we want her back. Says I, I will write her and see what she says. He says I wish you would.

I have been thinking about it all the afternoon and I could kick myself to think I did not settle it for good and all by telling him no with a big N, but he wants you to come so as to go to work Monday. But I have thought it all over and I don't want you to do it. But I told him I would write to you so I will write, but I don't want you to go to work on that job again just as you begin to feel like living again.

He says there will be no work to it at all, but we know better. It is more the nervous strain than the work that hurts you. I should have told him you could not do it in the first place and saved all this trouble in the begining. But I thought I would let you know which way the land lay. Don't think I want you to go to work because I write this. I want you to stay as long as you want to and have a good time and get strong and well. They will think no more of you if you accommodate or as much in the end.

134

. . . Can you get any dogs to bring back with you. We should have a dog or 2 or 3 or 4. Don't get more than fore dogs.

Now, Birdie, I want you to go right on enjoying yourself just as though I had not written this about Supt. Danniell. He can get girls if he can't get you at Manchester if he is a mind to send for them. I guess of course if you could do it it would be nice for you to get cashim but if we can't we can't and that is the end. So I guess they will be other ways of getting cashim besides doing work that we can not stand.

It will be nice if mother & Carrie could come down with you when you come back. We could have a sort of reunion. Wish Milton could come to. The peas are all budded, the cucumbers have got ther 3 leaves. We leave the kittens and Pot out in the shed days now, they are big half grown nearly.

Write as soon as you get this and give you refuseal to run Mr. Mayo machines to please me you understand what I am coming at. Love to all little girls.

Jinny

Alice to Gene:

West Randolph, VT, June 14, 1894

Dear Jin

We came up here to Carrie's Tuesday morning & yesterday Daddy came up & went jinsenging & got a six quart jar full & this morning he took the train & went up to Braintre & tomorrow we all go to Bethel & Saturday we go

135

up to Roswell Morgan's. Emma is enjoying herself as well as she can without her Dimmieman. After she read your letter she wanted to go right home. She is so affraid you are having a lonesome time and that the greasey dishwater will make you sick, but we tell her you wanted her to come & knew just how it would be without her & that you can get along.

I took her to Dr. Childs & she has given her quite a selection of medicine. I notice if she works much she is worse. Down at the Bascom House she acted real smart, up here she helped Carrie some & seemed worse, made her cough. We want her to stay until the last of next week & maybe Carrie will go down with her. Carrie has been real sick & looks awful bad & it may do her good. I wish Emmy could stay at the Bascom House all summer . . . I am glad Betty Ann's kittens can come up for six cats are better than 4. I think Emmy may bring down a six-toed cat & maybe a big hound dog.

Allie

Bethel, June 15, 1894

Dear Husband

We got back from Carrie's this afternoon on the 2 train and when Dadie came we found 2 big letters and the Bethel paper. It has got my name in it. Guess we will send it to you when we get it read. No prince, no men yet, the conductor on the train when we went up to Randolph tried to mash but it did not work at all, but he was pretty. We are going to Roswell Morgan's tomorrow or next day. Dadie got 6 or 8 dollars worth of root in 2 days up to Carrie's. Ed is a good man, I like him pretty well but no man like Dimie

136

man, little soft velvet sing.

You will have to tell Daniels that it is simply impossible for me to run those Mayos under any condishions, if it was not I should never give them up for I don't give up anything I can do and live. But I might as well jump in the river and drown myself, it would amount to the same thing in the end. Have not much more than got over my 4 days work. I should like to if I could but can't and that SETTLES it once for all. If he don't want me to wind pieces all right, can do something. Yes, take good care of your self and be good a while longer. Will write more soonly. Mama and Dadie send love. 4,000,000,000,000,000,000,000,000 kisses.

Your wife Emmy

Sat noon, June 16, 1894

My dear wife to come

It is awful hot here today. What do you think of that job running Mayo machines, it is to hard for you so I would not think a moment of doing it. There is lots of the girls going to quit on account of low wages and hard work. They will not stand it as soon as hot weather comes on, are going to be plagued for help I guess. Charles Hill talks of getting through if he can get a job down at his home. He is going down next Thursday to attend the mareage of his brother & will look about and try to get a job.

I received your letter and was glad to hear your decision in regard to running Mr. Mayo's machines in more ways than one. They are troubled to get girls to work, the reason is they won't pay a poor girl enough to make it any object for them. There is lots of girls working who are not absolutely obliged to and they will only work when they can

137

get good pay. So they have either got to raise or go without. They will be more pieces sometime. Lydia has got through, she quit in a day or 2 after you started for mother's. Oh, but it is hot, 102 on the piazza, too hot to cuddy. Had a good piece of calicoing for tonight but shall not take it, is to hot, aint I a good husband, true to Emma.

My dear Emma I want to see you awful bad but I hope you will not get in love with any man & not come back, leave poor dimmie man. I am going over to see your old love on Franklin Hights tonight and pay him that $10.00 if I can. I told you how I went over last Sunday and found him gone away.

It is awful hot tonight . . . Poor cats they all go downstairs now, thought I had lost them then called them & they did not come. Went low on stairs and called & they came out of cat hole. They are smart but is to hot for them to play tonight.

My dear wife to go, we are going to have a strawberry cake for supper, last one of the season . . . Who are you loving tonight Emma, that railroader or Dimmie man. Milt done well to get so much ginseng. Oh I wish he & I had the time to do the country all over. I think we could. We can look over Bristol and Enfield, that will give us some idea of how much there is to be had near here.

. . . Stay just as long as you want to Birdie, for we are getting along pretty good. Little Miss Holt has just gone home, should like to cuddy and kiss but scaired to death of Emma, Emma has a true man does not play when his Dear One is away, awful good man. Blowes his own horn to Emma bone tapper.

How is your cough got, well I hope. Take all the comfort you can and get rested and well because Dimmieman wants his Emma to feel awful good & rais the devil with Jinny.

Danniell will take my end off, am awful glad you

138

have settled it, you cannot run those machines, there is no use of talking about it any more.

Sunday morning

. . . The garden is fine, everything growing nice. We went over to Huntoons last night. Jim Vine came at 9 o'clock, Jim is working for Collins. His papa give him $10.00 that takes it down to half. Jim said he would take the hay at the same price as he did last year, not so bad, hey Berth. Mrs. Huntoon is not well, got cold worked too hard I guess . . . I guess someone broke in the barn up to Hill and stole a load of hay, quite a swipe is a load of hay to go . . . Have you had any cuddie Emma. Wish you were all here today it is a splendid day. The cats eyes do not look right, what shall we do with them.

Jinny

June 17, 1894

Dear Mother

I will write you a line, am awful glad Birdie is feeling so much better. You can keep her as long as you want to if Carrie does not want to come Friday. It is awful lonesome without her but can stand it knowing that it is doing her good. What I am coming at, I would not let her see pretty men because you know the girl is young and anxious for all men, may run off & leave the he.

Dolly & Jackey go out doors now, leave the cat hole open so they can circulate at will, keep them out in the shed

139

days now. Jack smelled the pan when he came in at noon.
You should mention I take more notice of Jack, he says the
cats are more consequence than he is. Poor boy, he is
sensitive like the rest of us, wants notice taken of him.

. . . You are coming back with Birdie ain't you, or
are you going to wait till daddy comes. Want to see you all
and talk it over. Has Emma seen all _____ yet, if she has not
don't let her, fraid she would run off and leave the he . . .
Will whitewash as soon as Birdie get back. There is no news
to write, love to all.

Jinny

Bethel, June 17

My own darling man

8 o'clock, ham and eggs for breakfast. How do you
feel this morning. It is a lovely one up here. A hard thunder
shower in the evening but not much cooler.

We had a good visit at Carrie's. You would not
know Ed hardly, he has grown good looking and a good
man. I wish you could see him, you and him would like each
other very much . . . Did Daniels get mad because I could
not run Mayo machines. What a chance to have seen Locke.
Wish I had come.

. . . We do have all the sewing one could do. Bell has
just brought up a sattine dress for mama to cut and she has
got a lot on hand . . . Ms. Childs has helped that trouble a
lot . . . Do you have to work just as hard as you did. How is
your stomach, better. Have you got any more medie yet. Ma
don't know of any dogs I can get but plenty of cats. If you
want any more let me know.

140

Well, if Carrie comes down with me shall be there 22 Friday so will write a line and tell you. Dadie went rooting yesterday and got some over a pound. Said he did not go over 5 miles. Pretty good we thought, he is lotting on coming down to hunt root and black bass with Genie boy. He thinks the Genie is a pretty good fellow to hunt with but says you have got to find your own roots.

Emmy

Monday noon, June 17 1894

My darling wife to go

It is hotter than hell today, is a shower coming up, had a hard thunder shower last night but it did not do much good to make it cooler. Dannell said he was sorry, he said you prejudiced against those Mayo machines, says she just ought to see them run, you would be suprised to see the difference in those machines. Probily you would if you run 3 of them.

. . . Yes, Milt must come after haying & catch a big bass, tell him I will try and find my own ginseng root. If I can shall try hard to find it so we can make a pot . . . What are you doing today, making a mash I suppose as usual. The cucumbers have clear up to the screen. Shall have to take the boxes off I guess.

Mike & Pat have a sort of a film growing over their eyes like Teddie boy had before he died, in his case I suppose it was caused by old age. But don't see what should cause it in the young cats. Can we do anything for them, it is not bad yet, may go away.

Jinny

141

June 18, 1894

Dear Jin

. . . Your dad went a fishing the other day but no
fish did he get. He brought me some water lillies. The circus
you went to did not come to Randolph as they intended. But
August 11 there is to be an awful big one Ringling Bros. an
awful menagerie, the biggist giraffe in the world, 3 rings &
all the wonders of the world, but we will not be here, for we
want to be in Franklin before that time if your dad can only
get around. He is so up to his ears in work all the time that
it makes me worry for fear we will have to wait. I want him
to get all around this next week coming so by the 5th or
very soon after we can start, I shall do my best.

There is an excursion to Ausable Chasm next
Tuesday. Just think, clear to New York state & acrossed the
lake for 1.50. But we would not go for I can't step very
lively on my sore leg. I think it is better today. I can't see
for the life of me what made it. Write soon, I want to see the
cats & the garden. This would be nice weather to be at the
farm.

Mother

Monday morning June 18th

Dear little Dimmieman

. . . Emmy is feeling lots better, last Saturday she said
she did not know when she had felt so well. The rest is
doing her so much good I wish she could stay six weeks.

142

Carrie has promised to go down with her & if she does they will come Friday, and if she don't I want Emmy to stay as long as she can. But she is so affraid they will want her in the mill & she don't want to lose her work.

But she wants rest as much as anything in the world, for as soon as she went to work up to Carrie's she commenced to feel bad and her [Carrie's] coffee was just awful. She has the same old coffee pot she had 7 years ago and it *never* has been washed. She can't keep house much like Emmy.

Your daddy went jinseng hunting yesterday & got a pound. He is awful busy now with the gardens & haying coming right on. How's Potum & Big Mike & Chakey on he pins & Dorothy [cats]. We want to see them awfully. How do you get along keeping house. We had ice creame Saturday, Katie Bascom made it, 10 cts a plate & then they had it for dinner & roast turkey. Emmy says she has seen some awful nice men, wishes she was not married.

Mother

Gene to Emma:

Wed. noon June 20, 1894

Dear darling wife to go

I saw that the potato bugs were hatching out so I shall have to Paris green them soon. I wish they would disappear for good, they are no good.

My dear wife, who do you love today. They had a wedding at the Catolic church yesterday morning, hope they will always be happy like the he and the she, don't you. Mrs.

Estray man got mad & quit at the paper mill last Tuesday, is going to St. Albans. Mrs. says she will be lonesome without her man. Perhaps she will cuddie with the he. Mrs. Estray went to Tilton yesterday & saw Dr. Osborne. He said you should not work, you are not fit to work. Says she, I cannot sit in my room all the time, I should fly all to pieces. Such kind of folks are awful sick all the time but seem to work & go out late evenings just like well folks.

Wed. eve

Dear wife to go

It is hot again tonight but not as hot as it was Monday. Am lonesome here without you. You should hear some of our arguments at meal times. Requires a lot of brain power you can bet your hat, but we are able to hold our own you know. We have talked about mill owners, why they cut pay and so forth.

Have just been down to see Mrs. Sawyer & get our watering pot. Robert is at home. Mary is coming tomorrow. The hefier is going to calve, she is fat, looks nice, will make a good cow. I guess I spoke about our taking the calf if it is the right sex to raise. It would be nice if Buttercup & the heifer should both have a girl calf & we could raise them both. Have a pair of good ones to go up to Hill to start in a great hurry if the bull is any good.

Thursday noon

. . . If we could get those calves & raise them they would make a good pair of calves. The pieces have not piled up as yet, expect they will 1 of these days . . . Shall look for you some tomorrow, my dear girl to go. The cats sit in the shaving & Jack got his fingers a holt of it. We loves them

144

very much, they are pretty, play good. Do you think Carrie will come with you or will she wait until you make a little longer visit in old biddie hen coop to go. Want to see Emma muchly to go. Mrs. Estray says her old man leaves her today, goes to St. Albans. She says she hates to have him go but she says she can stand it. Will mail this today so you can get it before tomorrow.

Gene

Carrie writes to Gene and Emma, so guess she came down with Emma after all:

West Randolph, July 5, 1894

Dear Sister and brother

I guess you thot it is time you herd from me so I will write you a few lines. Got home all right, Ed met me at the depot. He was glad to see me you bet. He said it was the longest time he ever saw since I went away. What did you do the 4th. I stayed to home all day and kept them away from fire crackers. Everything was quiet here as any other day, all but the children of course. They have to have some fun.

Gee whiz. This is a near day gone in the mill yet to work. Had a letter from mama, she is coming to stay all Sunday with me this week.

Well, I don't know as you can read this but I han't got but just a few minutes, the mail won't wait for me. I think it is a shame to hurry anyone so, don't you. Write soon. All send love. Frank is about the same as he was down there.

Tabbie

Alice to Emma:

Dear Emmy

The train you came up on the 6th of June has just
gone up with the usual terrible uproar, and I wanted Emmy
to come really. Mama's under the weather & am limpin. Last
Monday as I undressed to go beddings, there was a place that
looked like a pea just above my knee. It itched a little & I
thought no more about it. It wan't bigger than a pinhead &
the next day it was all swelled & awful sore & it has been
getting worse.

Miss Childs came in but she knew no more than I
did, so we had Dr. Clough come in. Your pa brought him
along when he came home, & he thought it was poisoned
some way. Said I might have scratched off the skin & my
nail might have done it, so he painted it with iodine and left
me some medicine for a tonic & said my blood & all of me
was out of order. So today I have to sit with my leg in a
chair & can only lay on my right side. It's on the left leg. It
looks to me as your ankel did when the spider bit you at
Hill. Tuesday night I was wild with the headache & Ephraim
kept that awful planner going till 1 o'clock at night.

. . . Belle has gone, she got so bold a calicoing that
she went around with no clothes on & did not do her work.
Mr. Dalzier the contractor for the new tanerry they are
building was going to leave if Bell went away & take all his
men, but he did not scare the Rolly, you see he loved her &
instead of the stately elms they had Room 18.

Oh, now I want to ask before I forget it do you have
Buffalo bugs, they are just awful here & at Randolph. One
woman killed 700 & it was no bug day either. You must

146

have had a hard time with the festive bed bug, Jack had his revenge when his mattress made your bed full.

This hot weather is helping the bugs & microbes. That Sylvester building where your dad got his death blow I am afraid sometimes that old water closet had been left till the building smells. Mr. Marston has been sick all summer & his boy has been taken with typhoid fever, but the Board of Health has got hold now. The man that lives there promised to take care of it so Sylvester never thought about it. It's where we bought the brush & thread, etc.

. . . I shall be there before long just as soon as I can get him started & I am in a hurry for he don't seem to feel very well, says he has that nervous hypo he calls it. My leg is better today.

Mother

Adelaide chimes in with a letter to Emma; the Gyppie she refers to is either a dog, cat or their horse. The couple did not have any children:

Bristol, NH July 29, 1894

Dear Bertha

I dont know when we shall get over to see you again for it is so hot we dont feel like doing anything when it gets Sunday . . . I want to know how you all are and what you are doing.

I have not been out of town yet. They talk of shutting down for repairs all summer and I thought they might the 1st of August, but they keep getting orders so I presume they won't till Dec. and then I shall have waited in vain and gone nowhere.

147

Did you go to see Allie? And is she with you now?
. . Have you been over to the farm this summer? I have been
thinking I should like to go over there after berries. I have
been after Raspberries twice up to Bridgewater but they were
not very plenty this year.

Lammie [Edward] is getting more and more plump as
the days pass, weighs 167. He feels the heat this summer
more than I ever knew him to and I think it will close me
out if it lasts. It seems to go to my stomach. I will be all
right when it gets cool. Gyppie is very much better. The best
she has ever been since we have had her.

Write me a few lines if you have time and excuse the
looks of this, my hand sticks to the paper every time I touch
it. Love to all from

Addie King

Alice to Gene and Emma:

July 1894

Dear Emmy & Son

Did you get the letter I wrote last Friday. It was sent
downstairs to mail & as I had not heard from you I thought
maybe you did not get it. I wrote you what an awful time I
had with the sore on my leg. At last I had Green come up &
he said right off it was a boil & I put on a flax seed poultice
& it soon fixed it. But it was just awful, I don't want any
more.

. . . We think we can come the first of next week. I
will not set a day & you can leave the key under the rug if
you all are in the mill.

Oh, Emmy, had I better bring my oil stove. We want

to go up to the farm & stay a few days, get someone to take us up when the blackberries are ripe & I thought maybe we would need my stove.

Gene to Alie:

Franklin, July 31, 1894

My dear mother

We received your letter & was glad to hear from you & that you was coming down so soon. You don't know how I & Birdie lot on your visit. It is to bad about your leg. Birdie had something like it, a spot swelled up on her leg & was awful sore but did not make her lame any.

I thought if you could come along about the 11th of August I could get out of the mill about that time 9 or 10, 11 any time for that matter, but thought it would be a little more convenient for me & prehaps for Milt as well.

Gene

Cooler weather has come and more troubles beset poor Milt:

Wed noon, last call, Oct. 2, 1894

Hims will try & write a line cause want the 2.00 to get to wifey soon. Yes, I cept to work on carpets devil & all & guess have got la grippe some if not more, anyway have got so I don't try to do anything but chores & even not working yesterday has made me feel lots better. So hope if keep still as can a coupple days more may get over it. You

149

see if I undertake to do anything I am just as wet as a rag, hawk & gag enough to chock a moose. Just as bad & so weak tremble all over then cold chills head feel bad ache.

Ally, hims knows if he had stoped in time it would not been so but no one knows how one is placed here, everyone howling to have something done & if one does not go to bed he is lost, then he has got to lock the door & let them pound untill they are obliged to give up.

It rained this morning & it was all I could do to stagger down & do my chores. Yet there were 3 that was shure that I could go into old damp cellers out of the rain & work cleaning old brick, sawing wood & the devil & all, & hims after the horse was stole & he had just about killed himself when he had ought to have been a bed for days. Got mad at last & told them that if they could not get anyone else to do their cussed damp nasty jobs they would never be done for I was going home to bed & I had 2 rifles & a 32 self acting deringer & I would shoot every dammed son of a gun that said work to me again for a week, and I felt just as I said. Everyone most has to say put the whiskey right into you Milt & you will be all right in 2 or 3 days. Oh such cussed fools, I wish they could take my place 24 hours, I should like to say put the rum in & you will be all right.

I have tried almost everything & of course whiskey. A little of it is good as far as it goes, but that is a small ways in my case. I am going to get another bottle of Hilions pills for they are no humbug where a cure becomes chronic or not. If I had commenced them as soon as I had the awful soreness in my throat, come & stuck to them I should be all right now I think, but can't tell & now got all used up. Think shall be lots better when get over it afore long.

Most time to get over to ofice, will write a line again soon. I honistly think if I keep still a while I will come out all right. So darling need not worry cause if it gets to bad shall have her come to keep me indoors & from being

150

dragged into some old carpet jaw or the devil knows what.

Awful sorrey about Sims & the trouble of the kind she has make awful work you know. And Mrs. Parker was agoing to die everyone thought until she saw an eye spec & he brought the whole case all right by her having the right glasses to wear.

This awfull mess has been big job for poor old hub but wifey will make it out someway. Hims got to be carefull now or he goes up sure so hers need not fear on that account.

Carrie writes Emma about work again:

West Randolph, Oct. 19, 1894

Dear sister Emma

How do you do I would like to know and why don't you write a fellow a little bit of a line to say you are well and happy. Ed has been real sick since I wrote you before but he is better now and has gone to work again. It don't agree with him to have his hands in water so much washing wagons. This cold winter weather is their only call for help in the mill, then we would both come if we could get work. Wouldn't it be nice to be all together. So Emma my plans fell through just as you said.

Is Mama with you now. How I want to see you all . . . Well they say I got to hurry as this wont be taken to office. I don't know as you can even read it I have hurried so. I wish you would see what you can do for me and Ed in the mill. If you can get us job work for the winter you shant lose anything.

Tabbie

Emily Cass writes a long letter to Emma:

Rochester, VT Dec. 12, 1894

Dear Niece Emma

You are wondering what has become of your aunt up in Vermont, so think I will write you and tell you she is still here . . . In July I had a tumor that laid me up or near so for a month and then when I got so I could ride and take some comfort Clara and I went to the village one day and I fell down some steps and struck my shin on a marble slab and hurt me terribly. It was done in Aug and never healed until the week before Thanksgiving and the scab never came off until last night. The Dr called it a fiberous tumor. I could not walk and had to go when I did step with a cane, it is very weak now. Have had the Dr at the house 3 times and need to see him more. Have not walked to a neighbor's since the very first of Aug and not to the hen house for weeks. Clara had all the cooking to do for a long time. I could sit and mash potatoes, do dishes and iron. At last we have got our house cleaned, papered and painted Clara's room and painted the middle kitchen floor.

And I still have news for you if Carrie has not written then to you, that I have a son but he is a great boy. Clara was married the 4th of Sept. to Ernest A. Hulett, son of Charles Hulett, the man that owns the creamery. They had been going together for near a year and as he had work here they wanted to be married. It came right when my leg was very bad so they went to Bethel and were married and went up north on a little trip. We like him very much, he is so pleasant. Clara thinks there never was such a being. He works at the village in a shop, came on his wheel right while it was good going, now walks.

Will has made him a fine offer to come on to the

farm with us but he is no farmer and don't think he can learn to be one so I suppose in the spring we shall have to give them up and they go to keeping house, which it don't seem as though I would have them do but I suppose I done the same thing and left my home for one of my own.

. . . Clara and I done all her dressmaking. Grandma Cass has been in Warren 2 months this summer to visit where she has lived so much. She was 87 last June and very smart for her.

. . . Will had a fine hired man through the summer. They done a lot of work beside farm work. Now he is alone, has got down lots of wood on bare ground, has killed 4 hogs and sold three of them since then, bought 6 pigs and two shotes, has 18 head of cattle counting a calf he is raising. He has 18 cows that are giving milk and coming in term 4 expected next month. We have 20 hens 2 roosters, one will die at Xmas for our dinner. Our milk goes to the creamery every other day. We have two silos, had 11 acers of corn this last fall, over 4 hundred bushel of ears, potatoes are a June crop with us and our apples we had to buy, and last year had lots of them and made cider. Eggs are 25 cents a dozen, we get only 5 eggs a day.

. . . Have you had good luck on the farm this year. I felt so sorry for Carrie that her little girl did not live. She felt so bad about it, and she had had such poor health all winter.

. . . They have the dam built and soon to build the power house for electric lights. Poles all set and some of the places of business wired and some of the houses. I don't think we will have them this year. They built a reservoir at the village last year and have a fine water system now. Clara and Ernest went to the Thanksgiving ball at Hancock and expect to go at New Years up here. They went to dancing school all last winter. What a long letter I have written you, I hope you can read it.

153

Emma writes to Milt and Alice, with murmurings of another little King to come:

Dear Mama and Papa

Well, how do you get along, good. Am glad you are taking comfort. So are we, allmost to much we think sometimes, but we never shall be so young again don't spose. Well, I have got my rug done and have just commenced on my night dresses. Am going to make 2 if I can run the machine enough. It makes my back ache so I had to stop and lay down this afternoon, but I have not sewed any on it since you [were here], only that black waist. Can't wear that only about 2 weeks more. Don't know what I shall get then, a wraper I guess, I can just pin that grey flanel one at the top but it won't button at all. I am feeling pretty well but get tired awfully easy for me. Don't like it when I want to do big swat (my word) of work but as Jin says we can't allways do what we want to.

Well, the postmaster Daniels has lost his wife, she was burried yesterday afternoon. She was Fred's mother you know so the mill did not run in the afternoon, and my Dimmie read and slept and got rested. He has got an awfull cold. It was malignant grip, at last phneumonia, the matter with her. Jin said poor Fred looked all upset and Frank has done nothing but cry.

You remember Nellie David, you have heard us talk of her, she has got a big boy for her baby. I expect some lively times next summer if we do all we planed out and the most of them in April as before, don't you. The ____ club is getting pretty friskey, don't know but will have to enlarge the building for it pretty soon.

Well, him just got some cider and put red pepper in it for his cold. Warm of him up. We got your good letter and the papers, will send you some more books when we get them changed. Good night and lots of love to you.

Berth

We lose a few years here. Emma gave birth to her second child Hugh in May of 1895. Subsequently, she had Dorothy in September of 1901 and Helen in November of 1904. Benjamin F. King had died in 1901. Milton had died in 1904; sadly, the ginseng business proved not to be the cornerstone of his and Gene's prosperity. Alice, who had no children of her own, was living with Gene and Emma in Franklin, Hill or Bristol, NH. Thomas King, who never married, was a patient in some facility for the disabled or chronically ill and evidently has a barrel of woe as his letter to his sister Alice explains:

North Boscawen, Nov. 15, 1909

Dear Neal

I will try and answer your letter. I meant to have written before but my hand is weak. How do you all do, do you keep well, and hope you are all well. It has been a cold summer, I have not much news. Mr. York died last spring and Carrie W. Willis died a year ago. How are the relatives? How are the people at Bristol and Aunt Emily.

I cannot walk so well, I cannot cross the room without a support. Have not been outdoor for 2 years. I stay in my room and read the books and papers. The man I room with stays in the smoke room days. I am glad to get back to my room after being in the hospital. I hate to go into hospital, they put me into hospital if I cannot go to meals, or if I get cold so that I cannot help myself. We have three meals a day. We have meat & potatoes at noon, bread & butter at night and cake or doughnut, tea or coffee, milk and oatmeal mornings. Beans & brown bread Sat. night & Sunday morning, the year arround the same change of meat every day.

The doctor says that I am getting worse all the time. I think that Dr. Drake is not altogether right about it. If I had the means I could go and get greatly helped. I wish that I could stop the progress of this terrible malady. The Dr. said that it was well advanced, and that is four years ago. But there is nobody to help me here. I am thankful to the Lord that I can get arround as well. One poor man is in bed and has to be lifted arround. One man has to take morphine, he groans with pain.

Fred Evans is superintendent now. Mr. & Mrs. Milton and daughters, 2 little girls, have gone back to Contoocook. We have a reading room. There is another building where some of the inmates stay. It used to be an insane asylum. This month has been warm. Please write an tell me all the news. I hope that you all keep well, I hope that you will come down & see me when you can. There are quite a lot of visitors here. Well must close for this time by sending love to all & please accept a share for yourself. Yours truly, with love

Thomas A. King

Rochester, VT, July 30, 1911

Dear Emma

 I am wondering if you have all dried up with the dry weather this summer, and awful hot weather now, it is something awful. One had no courage to do anything. Are you all pretty well. Will and I are usually well, he works in the mill all the time. Ernest and Clara moved to East Killingly Corner in the spring onto a small place. She has 75 hens and 115 chickens. Ernest is doing carpentering most of the time, likes very much. They seem a good ways from us but children will do so. Soon yours will go from the home nest. Are you having a good crop this year. I cannot tell you anything about farm life now, for we have none.

 The Bristolers will always be on hand for a big meal. She sent me a handkerchief & had to tell me how hard times & no work so she could not afford to do much. She had better not done that, it could not cost over 16 cts. Bob was outgrowing his clothes but he could not have any new ones this time. Oh, they are to tight for anything. She said the weather was so cold she could not come up to see me, I should have to come there. I wonder if it was as cold for me as for her. I thought that great for one that was so brave & never minded anything & did not believe in sickness or cold or anything.

Aunt Em

Dear Emma & Family

   . . . The 24th of July your Uncle was taken sick with a flebitis leg and he was confined to the bed 7 weeks . . . I took care of him over 3 weeks along, Dr. coming three times a day, when I was taken with a bad bowel trouble and had to have help but Clara came the next week. So she helped, she stayed 8 weeks and 2 days. Then she had to go home as Ernest was alone with near 200 hens and chickens.

   . . . We live in the same house we moved into when we came to the village to live. Expect to have to move next spring or buy. 10 houses went up here last year and 6 this and now not room enough for the families. The Lole business is increasing every week and more people coming in working on a railroad to the Lole mine now. The firm Will works for has sent off near 30 car loads of lumber in a few weeks.

   Well how have you all prospered this summer, have you ever moved and are the children well, your husband and mother and yourself. Have you raised lots of poultry. Clara has and has near 200 lots of pullets now. Some of them have laid. Eggs down where she is are 50 cents per dozen and 40 here and very scarce at that. I have not a hen, only the cat and he is part Angora, his nose and toes look silvery.

   I am feeling better now for I am getting rested. We know nothing about Carrie's folks for they never write, but do know Frank and wife have parted. Has Carrie been to see you this year . . . The children must be most grown up, they all grow so fast and we grow old just as fast. Your Uncle's sickness has aged him very much.

Your Aunt Em

Eugene to Alice from a hospital:

Franklin, Feb. 9, 1915

Dear mother

How are you getting on at the old homestead, I shall
soon be with you. The Dr. said he thought he could get me
out of the hospital this week. I sat up half of an hour
yesterday and feeling better every day. I am getting all of the
bed I care for this time. Dr. Smith came in yesterday evening
chewing gum to beat the band. I said to the nurse the Dr.
has not forgot his gum. She said he never was known to
forget gum.

Sunday J. W. Favor and lady called to see me and
while they were here Harry Walton and lady [Maude] called.
Charles Gordon called Saturday, he says Myra is not very
well. Charles looks about the same as usual. I have not seen
him sence he stayed all night at the Old Farmstead 24 years
ago, a long time between visits.

We had twins born here yesterday, the first Friday
night. There was one born and yelled every night since. The
nurse says last night she was going to throw him out.

Last night I was presented with a boquet of flowers
from G. W. Huntoon and wife and little Harrie and Bernard
Walton came in. Harrie is a real pretty boy. Maude wanted
to know why I did not let them know that I was in the
hospital. I told her no one knew till I was gone in our
neighborhood. Harry is working for B. B. Tobie this week,
has been working for the city. He wants to buy hens &
chickens, will pay 12-13 cents a pound live weight. I will let
you know 2 days ahead when I am coming.

Gene

Carrie Hatch to Emma:

Dear Sister and family

We went up to Fort Ethan Sunday to see Frank, he is mustered into foren service Wed 25 and expects to be sent away soon. I guess they will send off all the boys and leave us the old stuff. Well we got to stand it I suppose.

It looks as if we are going to get a nice day so you will find me in the wash tub if you call. How I wish you could. Just to see anyone makes you want to all the more.

Carrie

Hugh King had married Helen Kenney in 1917 and they lived in Bristol, NH. In 1919 Dorothy King married Lowell Wylie. I don't know where they lived then, but I can remember their driving over to see us in Concord in the early '30s, so it must not have been far, possibly Canterbury or Bow. In 1922 Dorothy gave birth to her daughter, Florence. They were unable to keep her, and Emma and Eugene adopted her. Some time in the middle 1920s, Alice Allen died.

Helen King, my mother, married Richard Hayes in 1925 in Somersworth, NH and they subsequently went to New York City, where I was born. He sent the following letter to Emma:

New York, NY Jan. 27, 1926

Dear Mrs. King

Just a few lines to let you know that Helen and I are the proud parents of a healthy nine pound girl born last night at 8 o'clock Jan 26 and that both Helen and the baby are doing fine. I took her to the Hospital Monday night at midnight and was down to see her tonight . . . the doctors and nurse say that it is a perfectly healthy child. The nurse let me look at the baby in the nursery tonight and said that all the other nurses were all crazy about the baby as it was so fat and cute and pretty . . .

Dick

They stayed in New York only a short time and then moved back to Concord and lived with Emma and Gene on the Hopkinton Road farm. Shortly after, Richard contracted tuberculosis and was in a sanitorium in Glencliff, NH. He never returned to the family. At the age of one, I had no memory of him at all. The first time I saw his picture was in 1980 when I was settling my mother's estate.

Eugene died in 1930 in Concord, NH. My memory of him is very vague, just a tall, thin older man lying in a bed with a bad case of pneumonia. Emma had moved him into the kitchen where he would be warmer. She brought him a glass of hot lemonade and he spilled a little on the sheet. I can still see the yellow lemon pulp on that sheet. Perhaps a few days later, I was aware of some strange people in the house, and a young woman who seemed to be taking care of Florence and me because neither Emma nor Helen was there. After a while Emma and Helen came back with another woman and they brought in large vases of flowers. One held tulips of such a striking dark red that I thought they were made of red velvet. It was only years later that I realized they had just returned from Eugene's funeral.

About a year later we moved from the farm into the city when Helen went to Vermont. By 1934 we were all together again in Rutland, VT.

Have never figured out just who Charles Allen was. Emma used to talk about him a lot but I was too young at the time to figure out any connection. (His son, Karl E. Allen, wrote my mother in 1944, just after Emma died, that his father had died on February 4, 1944.) At any rate, Charles wrote Emma just after WW II started:

Lebanon, NH, Nov. 12, 1939

Dear Mrs. King

    I have been thinking that perhaps I better write you just a line and say Greeting to you on your birthday Nov 18th. We are getting to be old people. I know so when I think Mrs. Allen and I have been married fifty five years come Sunday Nov. 19. At that time we were married at Bethel by S. A. Parker and took the train for Montpelier at eight forty. So next Sunday Nov 19 we will go to Montpelier on the train from Lebanon at seven a.m. Mrs. Allen has a brother that has been living there for some years. The grandson is still there. So we will make them a little visit and then return as I have fifty hens this winter to keep me busy.

    Clayton is not to good. Is staying at So. Royalton this winter. He has a family that he lives with that come from Rutland. He was down to see me yesterday and we expect him down for Thanksgiving.

    I think I have said enough for once, so will close by saying I hope you and yours have a good winter. Remember me to the family. Best wishes.

Charles H. Allen

Clara Emily (this may be Clara Hulett) to Emma:

No date, possibly 1938

Christmas Greetings to you all

 Do you know Emma it seems a shame to live so near
& never see each other. That comes of being busy as we are.
Thank God we're able to do it & not be like Carrie. I have
not seen her for a year, have only called at Leo's once. Every
moment seems to be filled. I went in to the candy shop over
to see Helen but she was out of town. I was over with
another dealer on business and had only a moment. Was so
sorry to miss her. Better luck next time. Love as ever

       Clara Emily

Rochester, VT Dec. 20, 1939

Dear Emma and all

 It surely seems strange to live so near and never see
or hear from you. I have not been in Rutland this year or
anywhere else for that matter . . . Did you know Carrie &
Ed are with Leo, have given up their home. Hear from
Hugh's folks now and then, everyone OK.
 I know you keep busy with 5 to do for, I do hope
you keep well. Christmas Greetings to each and all of you.
Much love.

       Clara Emily

163

Emma Hatch, wife of Leo Hatch, writes to Emma about her mother-in-law Carrie Hatch:

Randolph, VT Aug. 2, 1940

Dear Aunt Emma

I was very glad to receive your letter and knew well enough you are wondering how Mother is. Have tried every day to find time to write you but the days just aren't long enough when one is busy.

Mother rallied the day after you were here and her general condition is improved. Her left side is entirely paralysed and her mind is far from right at times. She did not sleep at all nights in spite of all the pills and capsules the Doctor gave her. So we are now giving her a hypodermic every night and the patient and nurse are both resting better.

. . . Father and Leo are fine and the girls are brown as berries. They have a grand time swimming at the Red Cross playground here.

I will try to do better at letting you know of conditions here, and do come over when you can. Love from all,

Emma [Hatch]

Wednesday, A.M. [Nov. 13, 1940]

Dear Aunt Emma

I received your special delivery letter this A.M. and have received your other letters. But things are so desperately

164

blue and discouraging over here I hadn't the heart to write to anyone about it.

I took care of Mother just as long as my health allowed me to. It was a cruel and terrible grind night and day. We all realize how hard it is for Mother to be laid low this way, but she is most unreasonable and abusive. Of course it is partly her mind, but she was always a high strung, ugly nature if things didn't go exactly as she thot they should.

When I caved in we moved her across the street where a lady takes elderly people. It takes both Mother's & Dad's state assistance checks every month to keep her there. It is a dollar a day and the checks come to thirty. So we have Father to care for & clothe beside all the rest of Mother's expenses.

In the six months of sickness Frank has been down just four times & helped to the extent of fifteen dollars. This last Sunday he came down & said they couldn't do anything more as he isn't working all the time. Without a child nor chick we know he could do considerable but Florence, his wife, never had any use for the folkes and just won't help in any way. Clara has been over twice and spent a day.

I have been flat in bed recently and had to keep Ella Mae out of school to do the work & care for Leah. As yet we don't know whether this will mean a trip to the hospital for me or not. So you see we are in rather desperate straits all around. We do hate to throw the folkes onto the town but on Leo's small pay it is most impossible to carry everything.

Well, so the situation is here. Am sorry I have not written before but surely you will understand. Love to all, from all

Emma B. Hatch

At one point, Emma, Helen, Florence and I drove over to Randolph to see how things were with Carrie. She evidently was in a very bad condition as she did not respond when Emma tried to talk to her. I am not certain when she died but it must have been in the early 1940s.

Emma became ill in late 1943. Dorothy, whose husband Lowell had died earlier in 1943, came to Vermont and helped take care of her as Helen, Florence and I were working in the store. This was wartime and we were working seven days a week. She died in June 1944, about two weeks after I graduated from high school.

Reading her and Gene's letters was like a revelation to me. The Emma I had known from my birth was an elderly, white-haired woman, and to think of her as a smart, working woman with a lively sense of humor just didn't seem to match. However, I am very glad that I was able to change my image of her through these letters. As Huldah noted, Emma was a "social little body" and I'm sure that the surviving members of the family will be able to see her in that light.

Hugh King's daughter Fay married Nelson Adams in Bristol in 1946. Hugh died in Laconia, NH in 1974. Florence King married John Bowker in 1958 and moved to Somerset, MA. John died in 1996. Helen died in 1979 in Rutland, and Dorothy died in Rutland in 1990. Richard Hayes died in Lewiston, ME in 1978. He had married again and had a son, Richard Arthur Hayes, Jr. It would seem I had a half-brother I never knew anything about. I chose to stay single.

INDEX